George H. Marcus

Functionalist Design

Arch. Marcel Breuer

B 33
Thonet

George H. Marcus

Functionalist Design

An Ongoing History

Prestel

Munich · New York

Photographic acknowledgments on p. 167

Front cover (background): Greta von Nessen, "Anywhere" lamp, 1952 (see colorplate 17)
Front cover (insert): Marcel Breuer, Armchair, 1925 (see colorplate 7)
Back cover (top): Coop Himmelblau, "Vödol" armchair, 1989 (see colorplate 20)
Back cover (bottom): Wilhelm Wagenfeld, Tea service, 1931 (see fig. 31)
Frontispiece: Marcel Breuer, Chair, 1927–28. From *Thonet Stahlrohrmöbel: Steckkarten-katalog*, 1930–31

Edited by David Krasnow

Prestel-Verlag
Mandlstrasse 26, D-80802 Munich, Germany
Tel. (+49–89) 38 17 09-0; Fax (+49–89) 38 17 09–35 and
16 West 22nd Street, New York, NY 10010, USA
Tel. (212) 27-8199; Fax (212) 627-9866

Prestel books are available worldwide. Please contact your nearest bookseller or write to either of the above addresses for information concerning your local distributor.

Cover design by Adam Volohonsky, Munich
Lithography by Karl Dörfel GmbH, Munich (black-and-white illustrations)
and eurocrom 4, Villorba, Italy (color illustrations)
Typeset by Reinhard Amann, Aichstetten
Printed by Wagner GmbH, Nördlingen
Bound by Auer, Donauwörth

Printed in Germany

ISBN 3-7913-1423-8

Contents

For Paul
an unexpected enthusiast

Acknowledgments

The publisher's reader, who remains anonymous and thus cannot be thanked by name, must be definitively acknowledged at a distance for the sincere and perceptive comments that helped define the scope and direction of this book. Richard Martin's enthusiastic reactions to a version of the "Machine Art" chapter presented at the Design History Forum in Chicago in 1992 encouraged me to continue pursuing the ongoing history of functionalist design. Two colleagues—more accurately, close friends who are also colleagues—Kathryn Hiesinger and Ralph Lieberman, read the manuscript, and their reactions and suggestions were much valued. David Krasnow's sensitive and meticulous editing, which clarified and strengthened the text, has also been much appreciated.

The following helped by answering questions, providing information or access to materials, or giving advice: Pierre Adler, Mies van der Rohe Archive, The Museum of Modern Art, New York; Matilda McQuaid, Department of Architecture and Design, The Museum of Modern Art; Charlotte Perriand; Holy Raveloarisoa, Library, Fondation Le Corbusier, Paris; Rona Roob, Museum Archives, The Museum of Modern Art; Masaharu Taneichi, Museum-Library, Musashino Art University, Tokyo; Evelyne Tréhin, Fondation Le Corbusier; Robert Venturi; Ian Wardropper, Department of European Decorative Arts, The Art Institute of Chicago; and Judith Zuidema, The Knoll Group.

G.H.M.

1 MAX BILL
Wall clock, 1957. Made by Gebrüder Junghans AG, Schramberg, Germany. Stainless steel and aluminum. Diameter 11″ (30.2 cm). Die Neue Sammlung, Munich.

Introduction

Functionalism—the notion that objects made to be used should be simple, honest, and direct; well adapted to their purpose; bare of ornament; standardized, machine-made, and reasonably priced; and expressive of their structure and materials—has defined the course of progressive design for most of this century. Never a movement or an "ism," and lacking a precise definition and a manifesto, this aesthetic has nonetheless become synonymous with what is modern, and its antitheses—ambiguity, ornamentation, individuality, and complexity—with what is postmodern. A Spartan attitude that favors stripping design down to essentials (fig. 1), functionalism was not originally allied to style, material, or context, and its purist criteria have been applied over the last century and a half to vastly different types of objects. Historically, however, they have been directed most often toward items made for use in the home, where the dangers of excessive ornamentation, flamboyance, and individuality were more likely to be lurking.

Functionalism is clearly rooted in mid-nineteenth-century England, yet the concept did not fully coalesce until well into the twentieth, when it was first recognized and then seriously considered by art critics and historians, such as Herbert Read in *Art and Industry* (1934)[1] and Nikolaus Pevsner in what has become the fundamental description of the phenomenon, *Pioneers of the Modern Movement* (1936).[2] These early historians of functionalism were its champions, particularly Pevsner, who viewed its triumph as inevitable, "the genuine and legitimate style of our century."[3] Having announced their position, these writers could hardly be considered objective, yet the force of their partisan view of functionalism and belief in its moral imperative has persisted, and Pevsner's work remains today the basic text on the early history of modern design.

Pevsner's book charts a linear development based on the accomplishments of a few individuals, linking the industrial architecture of Joseph Paxton's 1851 Crystal Palace in London with William Morris and the English Arts and Crafts movement, and then with Walter Gropius and the Bauhaus, the school of industrial design he founded in Weimar, Germany, in 1919. Pevsner's was a heroic but somewhat narrow vision of the flowering of modern design, a "teleological approach," as John Heskett described it,[4] that gave precedence to the Bauhaus as the torchbearer of modernism, and led to a blurring of distinctions that by the 1960s had fused functionalism and the school in Weimar into one and the same phenomenon.

"Functionalism," applied in this context first to architecture, was likened to "the biological concept of the adaptation of form to function and environment" by Fiske Kimball and George Harold Edgell in 1918. It embraced "the conscious endeavors in modern architecture to make the forms of individual members correspond to their structural duties, to make the aspect of buildings characteristic of their use and purpose, [and] to make the style of the time expressive of the distinguishing elements in contemporary and national culture."[5] This broadly defined term could have described much of the architecture of the early twentieth century that did not imitate historical models directly; it continued to be used loosely to refer to anything that seemed new and unconventional, and in the spirit of the modern age.[6] By the early 1930s, however, the definition was narrowed sharply by a group of writers who limited it to buildings of a certain type or style, in particular those made of reinforced concrete, with flat roofs, strip windows, and a liberal use of glass, such as the structures at the renowned Weissenhof experimental housing development in Stuttgart in 1927, and those featured in New York in 1932 in the Museum of Modern Art's International Style exhibition.[7] When Alberto Sartoris published his survey of "functional" architecture the same year,[8] he could illustrate 676 works drawn from twenty-five countries, from Belgium to Brazil and Germany to Japan, that met the severe standards he set for this genre; interspersed among them were examples of furnishings, particularly tubular-steel furniture designed by some of the same architects, that Sartoris and others with a similar outlook regarded as part of the same expression. While many different types of objects had long been considered functionalist by virtue of their utility, efficiency, and economy, the term now took on stylistic connotations and came to be applied only to those that shared a particular modernist look.

The history of functionalist design did not stop with the crystallization of this image and the creation of the iconic tubular-steel furniture in the 1920s and 1930s. Much of what we routinely think of as functionalism today has been filtered through a distinct aesthetic vision that developed in the 1930s, and through the trappings of a stylistic revival that fermented during the 1950s and emerged strongly in the 1960s, particularly in the United States. Seen in the postwar period as a clearly definable style reaching back uninterrupted to the 1920s, functionalism had in fact been recast with a conceptual and formulaic rigidity and a chaste spirit that strayed from the actuality, if not always the intent, of the earlier expression. The issue was further confused by the revisions that the architects Ludwig Mies van der Rohe, Le Corbusier, and Marcel Breuer made in reeditions of their furniture at this time; reflecting new technologies and their own changed attitudes, they quietly rewrote history through a subtle updating of their work. The revival was caught up in the postwar building boom and directed at a narrow group of corporate clients and patrons. It was also narrowly promulgated, emanating from a few individuals whose influence was enormous: an architect, Mies van der Rohe, whose buildings set a standard of extreme refinement and who introduced a style that was much emulated; a curator, architect, and loyal disciple, Philip Johnson, who invented a recherché aesthetic and went on to demonstrate its possibilities; and a businessman, Hans Knoll, and his wife, the designer Florence Schust, whose commercial savvy and practical design sense made furnishings available that lived up to the quality of their settings.

Familiarity with functionalism through its revival has led to the stereotypes and misconceptions that have marred much recent writing on the subject, and have made such popularizations as Tom Wolfe's scathing resumé of modern design, *From Bauhaus to Our House*,[9] particularly unfortunate. However trenchant his presentation of the failures of functionalism, Wolfe

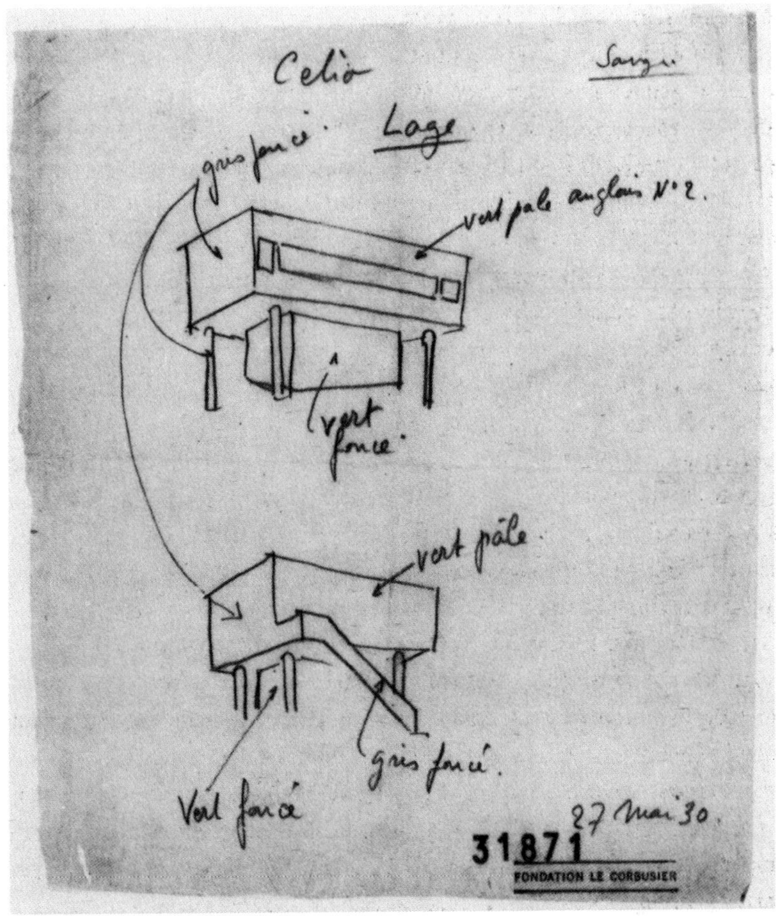

2 Drawing for the caretaker's house at Le Corbusier's Villa Savoye, Poissy, France, 1930, with indication of wall colorings. Pencil on paper. $10^{5}/_{8} \times 9^{1}/_{16}$" (27 x 23 cm). Fondation Le Corbusier, Paris.

misstepped by assessing the past in terms of a more recent period he didn't seem to understand. The work of the 1920s that he denigrated was both more thoughtful and more humane than he would allow, and if it wasn't accessible to the lowest class of workers as he expected it should be (and as some of its designers had intended it would be), it certainly aspired to be economical and available to a large middle class of consumers. Solid wooden furniture (much of it not unlike the simple, utilitarian, modular pieces broadly and popularly used today) and soft upholstered sofas and chairs appeared in the interiors at Weissenhof in 1927 along with the furniture "made of Honest Materials in natural tones: leather, tubular steel, bentwood, cane, canvas; the lighter—and harder—the better"[10] that Wolfe suggested was exclusively used there. Tubular-metal furniture itself was not necessarily icy and austere; much of it was lacquered and upholstered in colors beyond even the daring of many designers today (colorplate 11). Finally, Wolfe's contention that "inside and out," functionalist buildings "were white or beige with the occasional contrasting detail in black or gray,"[11] ignores the many integrated uses of color in the 1920s. The Bauhaus had a wall-painting workshop where multicolored painted decoration was planned,[12] while Le Corbusier, very much the Purist painter, created sophisticated color schemes for his buildings. The interior of his two-family house at Weissenhof had a complex program that included seven wall colors, from pale green and yellow to Venetian red and dark brown,[13] while the exterior of his Villa Savoye in Poissy was not to be completely white, as it has been iconically pictured, and its caretaker's lodge was to be defined by broad areas painted in shades of green and gray (fig. 2).

Because the term "functionalism" broadcasts the word "function" so boldly from within, it has remained bound to the idea that use should determine the form of an object, and that consequently, if an object is made to function well, it will by definition be beautiful. Discussion of this concept always begins with the famous dictum of the American architect Louis Sullivan. "It is the pervading law of all things organic and inorganic," he wrote, "of all things physical and metaphysical, of all things human and all things superhuman, of all true manifestations of the head, of the heart, of the soul, that the life is recognizable in its expression, that form ever follows function. *This is the law*."[14] This has suggested to many that a determining factor establishes one right and aesthetically pleasing form for each need, a Platonic ideal of a universal, satisfying type, which the designer can derive by charting all the uses and functions of an object. But a rock and a wooden plank work equally well for sitting on, and depending upon the diverse forms in which the human body comes and on the variety of human cultural habits, each may be deemed as comfortable as a soft upholstered sofa or a tubular-steel lounge chair.

3 ANNI ALBERS
Wall hanging, 1926. Made at the Bauhaus weaving workshop, Dessau. Cotton and synthetic fibers. 68 7/8 x 46 1/2" (175 x 118 cm). Bauhaus-Archiv, Berlin.

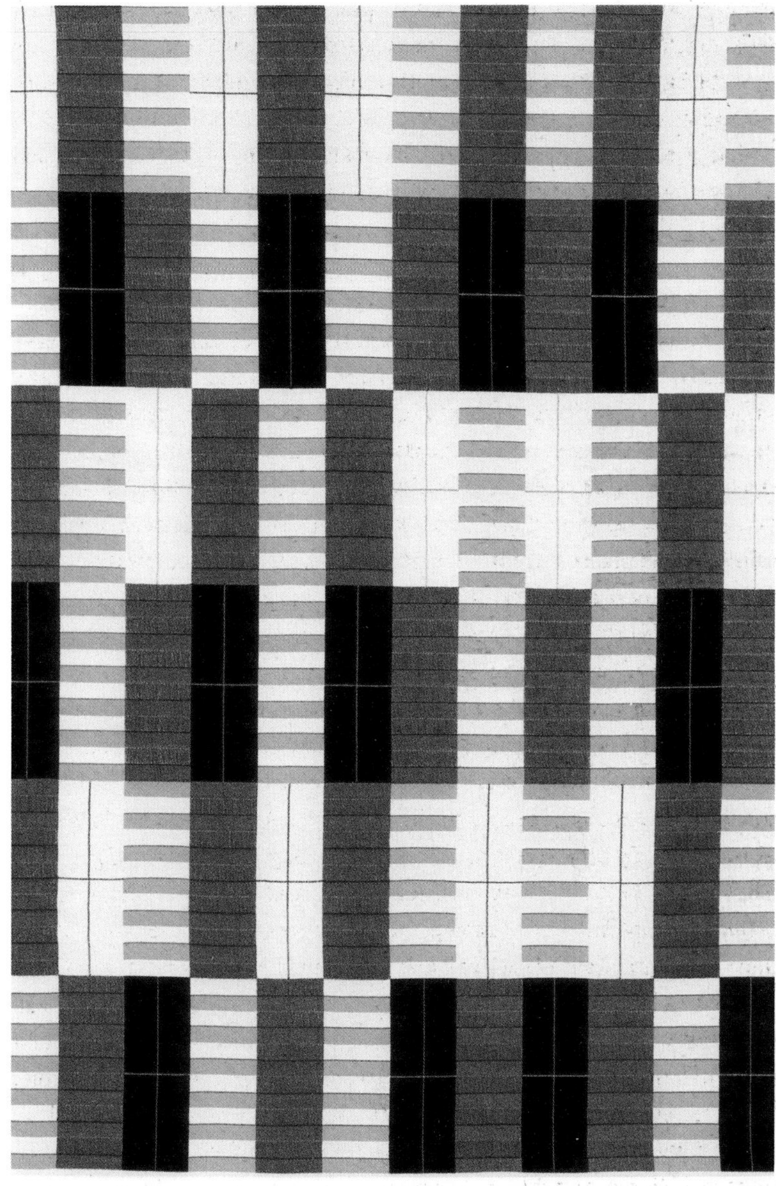

Functional determinism is not what Sullivan was getting at. His words were more specifically directed, and must be appreciated in context. Sullivan was promulgating the idea that form should express function or structure (rather than be determined by it), manifest in feats of engineering or in architecture by revealing, or suggesting, the supporting elements of a building or its interior divisions. His passage appears in a discussion of the aesthetic need for a "true normal type"[15] of skyscraper with a standardized system of articulation that would express on the exterior the separately functioning divisions of the space within. The expression of function in design is most easily illustrated by the technique of weaving (fig. 3), where the fibers of the warp and weft visibly create a pattern as they intersect to form the structure of the fabric; such patterns were virtually the only ones that came to be accepted by doctrinaire functionalist thinkers, such as Herbert Read, who in *Art and Industry* announced emphatically, in capital letters: "Appropriate ornament arises naturally and inevitably from the physical nature of a material and the processes of working that material."[16]

Those who strictly followed this definition of functionalism dismissed aesthetics as a determining factor; Walter Gropius, taking a somewhat broader view of function, added beauty as one of its components: "An object is defined by its nature. In order, then, to design it to function correctly—a container, a chair, or a house—one must first of all study its nature; for it must serve its purpose perfectly, that is, it must fulfill its function usefully, be durable, economical, and 'beautiful.'"[17] What Gropius and the other functionalist architects and designers did not recognize nor admit was that there were also symbolic aspects to their work, as Robert Venturi, the oracle of postmodernism, and Denise Scott Brown sympathetically pointed out:

> Functionalist architecture was more symbolic than functional. It was symbolically functional. It represented function more than resulted from function. It looked functional more than worked functionally. This was all right because architecture has always been symbolic.... The content of functionalist architecture was all right too because function was a vital symbol in the cultural context of the 1920s. But the symbolism of functionalist architecture was unadmitted. It was a symbolism of no symbolism: the functional image of a building was to result from the automatic and explicit expression of program and structure.... Aesthetic qualities, if ever mentioned, were said to derive from the easy resolution of the never contradictory functional requirements of program, structure and at a later period, mechanical equipment.[18]

Functionalism, many critics have suggested, is a style that is spent. The frequent pronouncements of its death are, however, based on the outlook and output of a privileged echelon of designers who have more recently chosen to follow paths of ornamentalism and referential design. Yet, in spite of having been reviled and rejected throughout the last decades, it remains a benchmark against which much design is judged. Its precepts and the style it engendered have endured, and over half a century later have filtered down to a popular level. Classic metal furniture designs, be they authorized editions or copies, have become more widely available, while a host of works that mine its utilitarian principles have now become commonplace.

Notes

1 Herbert Read, *Art and Industry: The Principles of Industrial Design* (London: Faber and Faber, 1934).
2 Nikolaus Pevsner, *Pioneers of the Modern Movement: From William Morris to Walter Gropius* (London: Faber and Faber, 1936). It was revised and reissued in 1949 as *Pioneers of Modern Design* (New York: The Museum of Modern Art), and revised again in 1960 and 1975 (Harmondsworth: Penguin Books).
3 Ibid. (1949), p. 18. Pevsner's fervor was not immediate; in the first edition (1936) he timidly described it as "a genuine and adequate style of our century" (p. 41).
4 John Heskett, *German Design, 1870–1918* (New York: Taplinger Publishing Company, 1986), p. 7.
5 Fiske Kimball and George Harold Edgell, *A History of Architecture* (New York and London: Harper and Brothers Publishers, 1918), p. 499.
6 Pevsner did not rely on the term "functionalism" in his book, referring instead back to the early twentieth-century use of "the untranslatable [German] word *sachlich*, meaning at the same time pertinent, matter-of-fact, and objective" (1975, p. 32). "Functionalism" soon, however, became the standard translation of *Sachlichkeit*, despite its common and less loaded equivalent "objectivity."
7 New York, The Museum of Modern Art, "Modern Architecture: International Exhibition," 1932. The term "International Style" appeared in the title of the accompanying book by Henry-Russell Hitchcock and Philip Johnson, *The International Style: Architecture since 1922* (New York: W. W. Norton and Company, 1932).
8 Alberto Sartoris, *Gli elementi dell'architettura funzionale: sintesi panoramica dell'architettura moderna* (Milan: Ulrico Hoepli, 1932).
9 Tom Wolfe, *From Bauhaus to Our House* (New York: Farrar Straus Giroux, 1981).
10 Ibid., p. 32.
11 Ibid., p. 22.
12 See Clark V. Poling, *Bauhaus Color* (Atlanta: The High Museum of Art, 1975).
13 See Karin Kirsch, *The Weissenhofsiedlung: Experimental Housing Built for the Deutscher Werkbund, Stuttgart, 1927* (New York: Rizzoli, 1989), p. 116.
14 Louis H. Sullivan, "The Tall Office Building Artistically Considered," *Lippincott's Magazine* 57 (March 1896), p. 408.
15 Ibid., p. 404.
16 Read, *Art and Industry*, p. 153.
17 Walter Gropius, "Bauhaus Dessau—Principles of Bauhaus Production" [1926]; translated in Hans M. Wingler, *The Bauhaus: Weimar Dessau Berlin Chicago* (Cambridge, Mass., and London: The MIT Press, 1969), p. 109.
18 Robert Venturi and Denise Scott Brown, "Functionalism, Yes, But," statement for the symposium "The Pathos of Functionalism," Berlin, 1974, in *Architecture and Urbanism* 47 (November 1974), p. 33.

Plates

1 MARIANNE BRANDT Tea infuser, 1924.
Made at the Bauhaus metal workshop, Weimar.
Silver and ebony. Height 2 7/8" (7.3 cm).
The British Museum, London.

2 MARIANNE BRANDT Tea infuser, 1924.
Made at the Bauhaus metal workshop, Weimar.
Brass with silver-plated interior and ebony. Height 3" (7.5 cm).
Bauhaus-Archiv, Berlin.

3 KARL J. JUCKER AND WILHELM WAGENFELD
Table lamp, 1923–24. Made at the Bauhaus metal workshop, Weimar. Glass, nickel-plated brass, and steel. Height 15″ (38 cm). Bauhaus-Archiv, Berlin.

4 ADOLF G. SCHNECK
Chairs from *Die Billige Wohnung* series, 1927.
Made by the Deutsche Werkstätten, Hellerau (Dresden).
Height of chairs 33½″/21¼″ (85/54 cm).
Kunstgewerbemuseum Berlin.

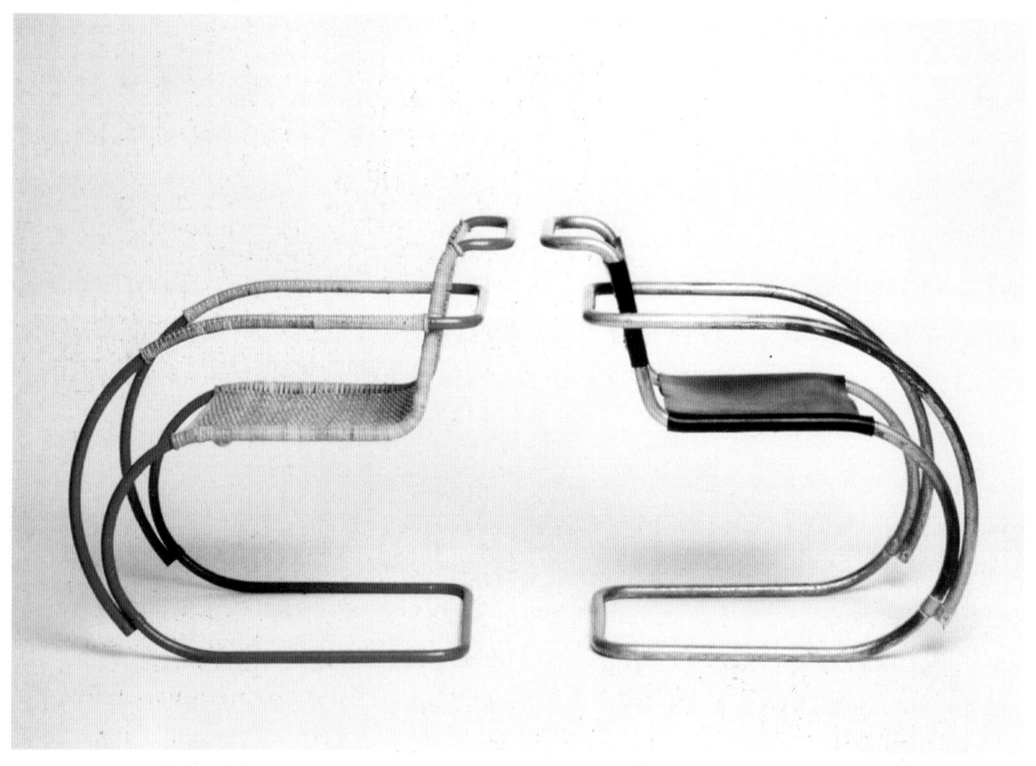

5 LUDWIG MIES VAN DER ROHE Armchairs, 1927.
Made by Berliner Metallgewerbe Joseph Müller, Berlin.
Lacquered steel, leather, and caning. Height approx. 31" (79 cm).
Private collection.

6 MARCEL BREUER
Nesting tables, c. 1926.
Made by Standard-Möbel.
Nickel-plated steel and lacquered wood. Height of tallest table 23¾″ (60.2 cm).
Bauhaus-Archiv, Berlin.

7 MARCEL BREUER
Armchair, 1925.
Made by Standard-Möbel, late 1927 or early 1928.
Chrome-plated steel and canvas.
Height 28⅛″ (71.4 cm).
The Museum of Modern Art, New York. Gift of Herbert Bayer.

8 LE CORBUSIER Villa Church, 1928.
Pencil and pastel on paper. 25 5/8 x 43" (65 x 109 cm).
Fondation Le Corbusier, Paris.

9 LE CORBUSIER, PIERRE JEANNERET, AND CHARLOTTE PERRIAND
Chaise longue, 1928. Made by Embru-Werke AG, Zurich.
Steel, iron, fabric, and leather. Height 26" (66 cm).
Fischer Fine Art, Ltd., London.

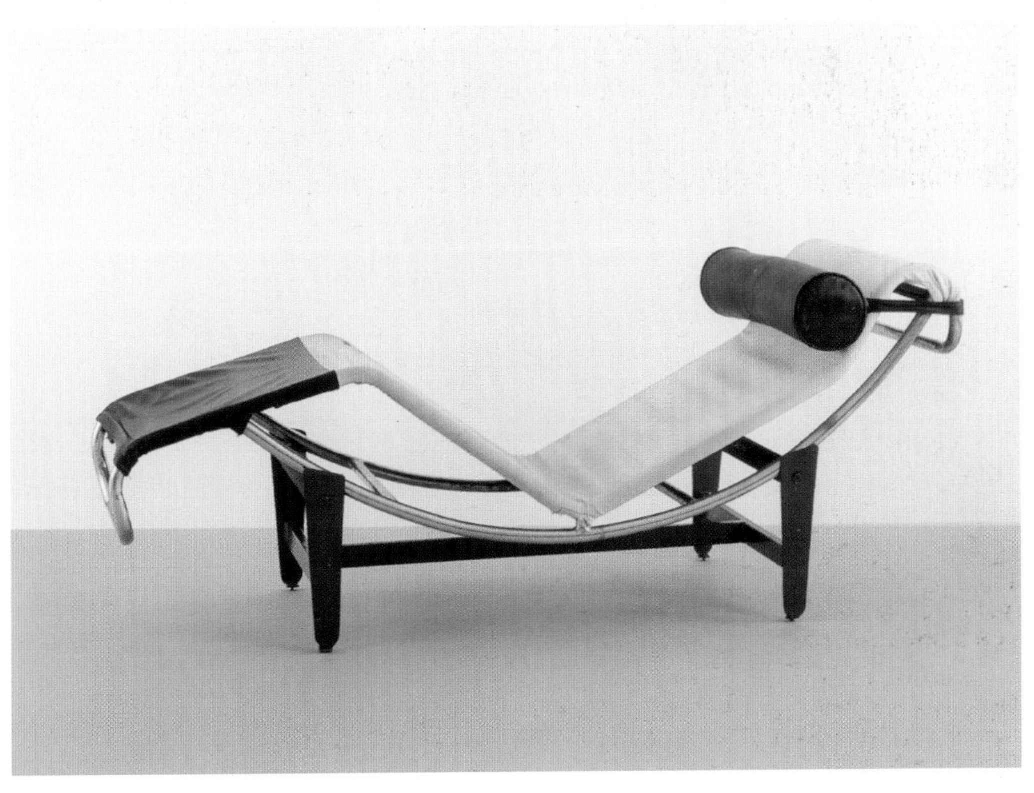

10 CHARLOTTE PERRIAND
Dining room, Salon des Artistes Décorateurs, 1928.
From *Art et Décoration* (June 28, 1928).
Victoria & Albert Museum, London.

11 Brochure for Marcel Breuer's *Stahlmöbel* (steel furniture), Thonet-Mundus (1931). Collection of Albrecht Bangert, Munich.

12 MARCEL BREUER
Armchair, 1925.
Made by Standard-Möbel or Gebrüder Thonet, c. 1929.
Lacquered steel and canvas.
Location unknown.

13 LUDWIG MIES VAN DER ROHE Chair, 1929. Made by Bamberg Metallwerkstätten, Berlin-Neukölln. Chrome-plated steel and leather. Height 29¾" (75.5 cm). Sold at Christie's, Amsterdam, October 1989.

14 LUDWIG MIES VAN DER ROHE
German pavilion, Exposición Internacional, Barcelona, 1929 (reconstruction).

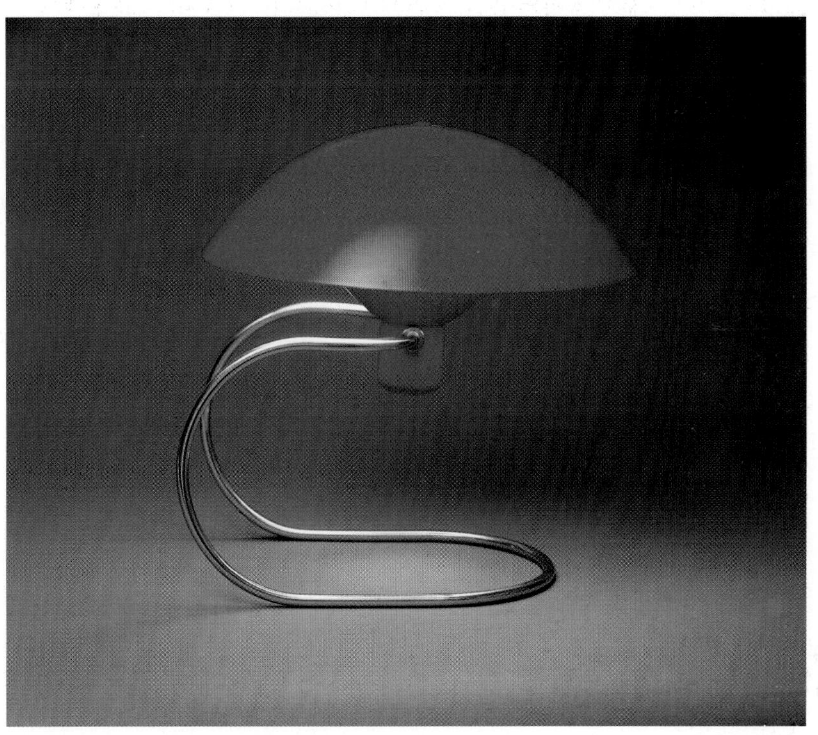

17 GRETA VON NESSEN "Anywhere" lamp, 1952.
Made by Nessen Lamps, New York. Aluminum and enameled metal. Height 14″ (35.5 cm).
Philadelphia Museum of Art. Gift of Nessen Lamps Inc.

Above left:
15 FLORENCE KNOLL Executive reception room,
CBS building, New York, 1962.

Below left:
16 GEORGE NELSON "Sling" sofa, 1964.
Made by Herman Miller, Zeeland, Michigan.
Chrome-plated steel and neoprene with leather-covered urethane-foam upholstery.
Length 87″ (221 cm). Herman Miller, Incorporated, Zeeland, Michigan.

18 ALESSANDRO MENDINI
"Redesign of Modern Movement Chairs: Wassily by Breuer," 1978.
Chrome-plated steel and painted leather.
Collection of Alessandro Mendini, Milan.

19 LE CORBUSIER, PIERRE JEANNERET, AND CHARLOTTE PERRIAND
"Grand Confort" sofa, 1928,
from the current Cassina production.

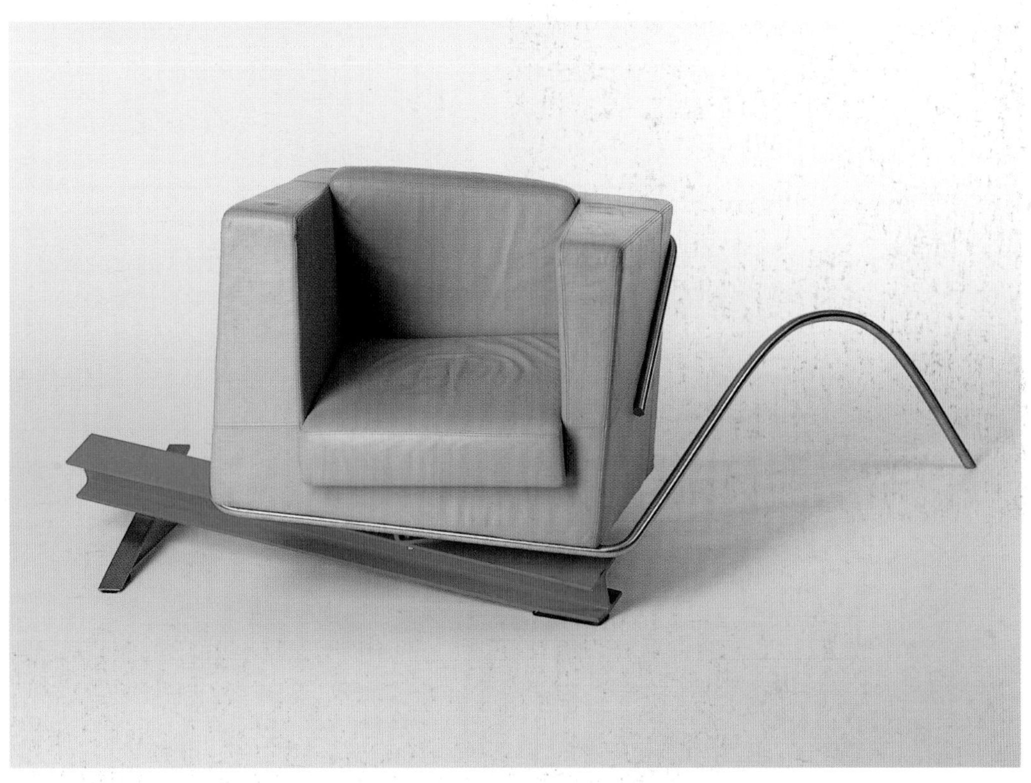

20 COOP HIMMELBLAU "Vödol" armchair, 1989.
Chrome-plated and painted steel and vinyl. Height 29½" (75 cm).
Vitra Design Museum, Weil am Rhein, Germany.

21 Mies van der Rohe exhibition,
The Museum of Modern Art, New York, 1977.

Fitness for Purpose

"But is a dung-basket beautiful?"
"Yes, by Zeus," replied Socrates, "and a golden shield is ugly—
if the dung-basket is well made for its purpose,
and the golden shield is poorly made."
Xenophon[1]

Just as Socrates found a dung-basket beautiful because of how well it fulfilled its function, the mid-nineteenth-century English *Journal of Design* praised a coal scuttle (fig. 4) as "an illustration of the improvement every object gains, even in the condition of beauty of line, by being first of all thoroughly well adapted to its purpose."[2] Such congruency of attitude expressed by two very distant sources does not mean, however, that aesthetic attention was paid to common utilitarian objects during the many centuries in between. Aesthetic guidance was directed instead to more lofty endeavors, to architecture, sculpture, and painting, following principles drawn from such abstract provinces as Platonic ideals, spirituality, logic, and mathematical proportions, rather than from utility. But the question of function and fitness did not cease to be of interest,[3] and with the appropriation in the nineteenth century of the

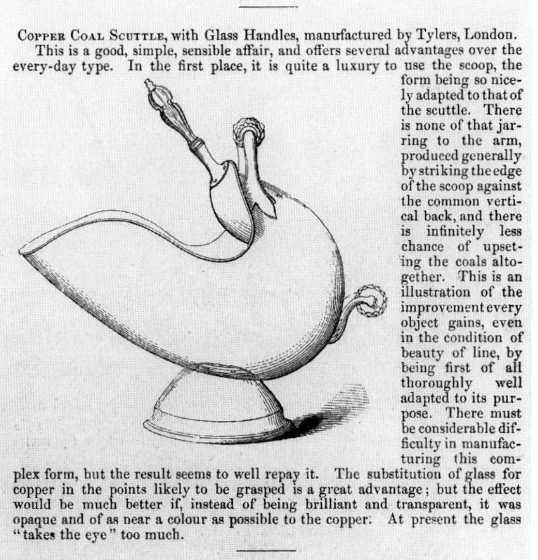

Copper Coal Scuttle, with Glass Handles, manufactured by Tylers, London.

This is a good, simple, sensible affair, and offers several advantages over the every-day type. In the first place, it is quite a luxury to use the scoop, the form being so nicely adapted to that of the scuttle. There is none of that jarring to the arm, produced generally by striking the edge of the scoop against the common vertical back, and there is infinitely less chance of upsetting the coals altogether. This is an illustration of the improvement every object gains, even in the condition of beauty of line, by being first of all thoroughly well adapted to its purpose. There must be considerable difficulty in manufacturing this complex form, but the result seems to well repay it. The substitution of glass for copper in the points likely to be grasped is a great advantage; but the effect would be much better if, instead of being brilliant and transparent, it was opaque and of as near a colour as possible to the copper. At present the glass "takes the eye" too much.

4 Copper coal scuttle with glass handles. From *The Journal of Design* (August 1849). The Metropolitan Museum of Art, New York, Library.

so-called decorative arts by forces of an industrialization bent on taking the greatest commercial advantage of ornamentation, and the resuscitation of the status of the decorative artist in response,[4] the legitimacy of functional suitability in aesthetic judgments began to be debated anew. It was the English Victorian reformers, practical proponents of restraint in ornament, who laid claim to utility once again as a factor in assessing the quality of design. Their immediate inspiration came from the writings of the Gothicist A. W. N. Pugin, who on the very first page of his architectural treatise *Contrasts*, published in 1836, proclaimed "that the great test of Architectural beauty is the fitness of the design to the purpose for which it is intended."[5]

It has become conventional, and convenient, to view the "Great Exhibition of the Works of Industry of All Nations," held in the Crystal Palace in London in 1851, not only as a demonstration of high Victorian taste but also as a battleground for functionalist principles.[6] Certainly Joseph Paxton's 1,848-foot-long glass and iron structure that housed it (fig. 5) was the most celebrated and most visible example of nineteenth-century functionalist architecture. Erected from prefabricated modular sections made of industrial materials, this much-imitated landmark expressed its almost evanescent fabric openly and simply and with little reference to the profuse ornamentation of the exhibits within, which was looked upon as suspect by progressives at this time. But the Great Exhibition stood as a monument to the tumultuous achievement of the industrial revolution, the several critical essays and reports on the state of design included in exhibition publications and reviews notwithstanding.[7] The exhibition was an omnium-gatherum of the products of international industry on all levels, an encyclopedic presentation of everything from foodstuffs to finery, from chemicals and surgical instruments to ceramics and tapestries. Following the nineteenth-century mania for classification, these were exhibited, judged, and premiated in thirty classes, subsumed under the headings raw materials, machinery, manufactures, and fine arts, and divided into more and more specific subcategories, as had been done at the series of French expositions of industrial manufacture on which the concept of the Great Exhibition was based.

Criticism of design at the exhibition centered on the area of manufactures, in which ornamentation predominated and objects were often conceived more with regard to the elaboration of forms and embellishment of surfaces than to utility. Faced with a preponderance of exhibits that pressed extreme, imitative naturalism into exceedingly imaginative formats (fig. 6) and applied high-spirited renditions and reinterpretations of historic styles to every manner of thing (fig. 7), critics of a utilitarian, reformist bent such as Richard Redgrave, a Royal Academician and author of the official exhibition *Report on Design*, lamented the reversal of the "rule" that ornament "cannot

5 JOSEPH PAXTON
Crystal Palace, London, 1851.

be other than secondary." This he "found to be the leading error in the Exhibition, an error more or less apparent in every department of manufacture connected with ornament, which is apt to sicken us of decoration, and leads us to admire those objects of absolute utility (the machines and utensils of various kinds), where use is so paramount that ornament is repudiated, and, fitness of purpose being the end sought, a noble simplicity is the result."[8]

As Redgrave's words make very clear, his concerns were directed at a particular context, "every department of manufacture connected with ornament," which he hoped might be induced to adapt the principles of utilitarian design demonstrated in the other classes at the exhibition. The fact that many simple and fit objects were already being produced, sold, and used without fanfare in commercial settings or in the most basic aspects of household management in England was not his immediate concern. For Redgrave, such articles, which from machinery to majolica had multiplied inordinately by the mid-nineteenth century with expanding mechanical production,[9] were a matter apart: they never aspired to the category of the ornamental arts and manufactures. In attacking the decorative arts, Redgrave was seeking to impose a new progressive taste on the millions of articles of manufacture then being flamboyantly ornamented in the manner favored by the increasingly numerous and affluent members of the consumer classes. Taking a paternalistic attitude, he feared that "without some critical guidance, some judicial canons, or some careful separation of the meretricious from the beautiful, it is to be feared that the public taste will rather be vitiated than improved by an examination of the Exhibition."[10]

The guidance and canons for the reform of ornamental design such as Redgrave espoused and later formalized in his "General Principles of Decorative Art,"[11] which joined utility and economy with a program of chaste decoration, had already been made available in *The Journal of Design*. A magazine of modest scale but grand vision and reformist fervor founded in 1849, it became the first arena for a programmatic discussion of what may be seen as modern design issues. Along with its articles on such subjects as ornament, design and botany, copyright laws, and the curriculum of the schools of design, and its reviews of international exhibitions of decorative arts, the monthly offered extensive discussion and criticism of objects newly on the market, which were illustrated in the form of engravings, or included when possible as actual samples pasted into each issue—calicoes, chintzes, book-binding cloth, machine embroideries, wallpapers, and other swatches from

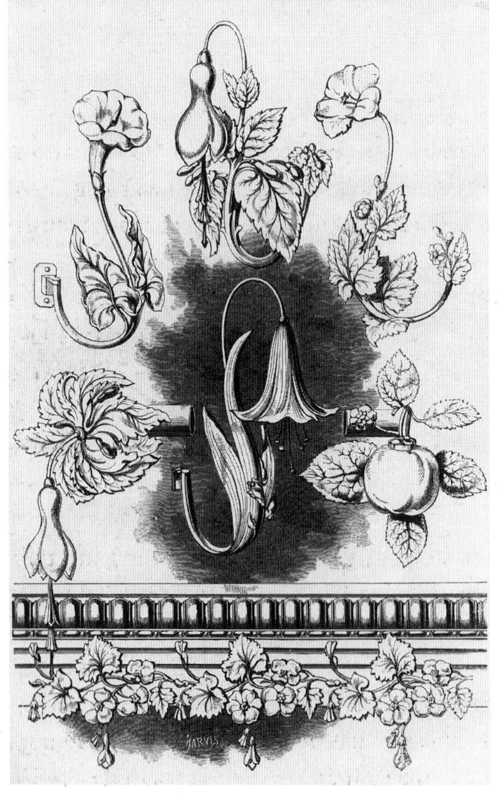

6 Group of curtain-bands, curtain holders, cornice-ends, and cornice, in stamped brass, with glass ornaments, representing lilies, fuschias, and mallows. Made by R. W. Winfield, Birmingham. From *Great Exhibition of the Works of Industry of All Nations, Official Descriptive and Illustrated Catalogue*, vol. 4: *Supplementary Volume* (London, 1851). The Metropolitan Museum of Art, New York, Library.

7 Group of patent piano-fortes. Made by Collard and Collard, Cheapside, England. From *Great Exhibition of the Works of Industry of All Nations, Official Descriptive and Illustrated Catalogue*, vol. 4: *Supplementary Volume* (London, 1851). The Metropolitan Museum of Art, New York, Library.

English and foreign manufacturers. The *Journal*'s aim was "to foster ornamental art in all ways";[12] a pragmatic publication, it was devoted to the business of manufacture and furthering the artistic quality of manufactured goods destined for popular use, as was stated in the first number: "We desire to exhibit and criticise not so much the best and most costly productions, and therefore exclusive patterns, but the *fair average* character of our manufactures, not neglecting the *very cheapest*"[13] (fig. 8). It later warned: "It is the worst of all mistakes to imagine that because a thing is cheap the artistic finish of its design is unimportant, since it is in exactly the ratio of its probable dissemination among the public that the influence on popular taste must be effected."[14]

The force behind *The Journal of Design* was Henry Cole, a longtime public servant and one of a notable breed of Victorian polymaths who broadly championed innovative programs for the betterment of society and the advancement of British industry, ranging from the reform of the British patent laws and establishment of the penny postal system to the efficient organization of the railways.[15] A major supporter and organizer of the 1851 exhibition, and a great devotee of its patron, Prince Albert, Cole later became the first di-

8 Cheap English paper-hangings. Made by W. B. Simpson, London. Sample inserted into *The Journal of Design* (March 1849). The Metropolitan Museum of Art, New York, Library.

rector of the Museum of Ornamental Art in London (which would become the South Kensington and then the Victoria and Albert Museum).

Cole had himself taken direct, practical steps to set an example for applying revitalized principles of design to industrial production. In 1846, using the pseudonym Felix Summerly—under which he had published a series of children's books illustrated by members of the Royal Academy—he won a silver medal in a Royal Society of Arts competition for the design of an ordinary ceramic tea service (fig. 9). Cole's plainly stated goal for the service, a combination of well-considered utility and economy, was

> to obtain as much beauty and ornament as is commensurate with cheapness. A higher standard in the ornamental parts would have led to much greater cost. The forms in principle are new combinations of those of the best Etruscan Pottery [which he had seen in the British Museum], with ornaments at the handles, &c., super-added and designed so as not to interfere with the simplicity of the outlines. The Cup being *deep* rather than *wide*, offers least scope for the radiation of heat and will keep the tea warm. The Milk Pot has three lips like some articles of Etruscan Pottery, enabling the liquid to be poured at both angles, right and left, which requires only a motion of the wrist.[16]

Cole had seen this award as the moment to launch an association of manufacturers, designers, and artists, which he called Summerly's Art Manufactures (a term he devised "meaning Fine Art, or beauty applied to mechanical production"[17]). The association, as it announced in 1847, aimed "to produce in

9 FELIX SUMMERLY (HENRY COLE)
Tea service, 1846. Made by Minton and Company, Staffordshire, England. Glazed earthenware. Height of teapot 6¼" (15.9 cm). Victoria & Albert Museum, London.

each article superior utility, which is not to be sacrificed to ornament; to select pure forms; to decorate each article with appropriate details relating to its use, and to obtain these details as directly as possible from nature."[18] The appropriateness of ornament and its basis in nature, the last of these aims, was a particularly nineteenth-century conceit that asked decoration to announce the purpose of an object, such as grape vines on a wine glass or, as in Redgrave's "Well Spring" jug (fig. 10), one of Summerly's products, reeds and rushes on a container for water. Mottoes, narrative scenes, motifs from nature—all could be applied when appropriate to communicate the purpose of an object on a visual and symbolic level.

The Journal of Design was an extraordinary publication not just for its unprecedented attitudes and goals but also for the strictness with which it adhered to its ideological principles and the doggedness with which it applied itself to the critique of design. Its pages did not hesitate to be critical whenever it found lapses or excesses, even in the varied products of Summerly's own art manufactures,[19] or, more astoundingly, in the design of a gilt centerpiece by the amateur Prince Albert, Cole's patron, to whom the first volume of the *Journal* was dedicated.[20]

Several years after the demise of the magazine and the close of the Great Exhibition, Cole again boldly confronted design transgressions—and the wrath of the manufacturing community—when as a museum director he publicly exhibited objects deemed to be designed on "false principles."[21] This was satirized in a review in Charles Dickens's weekly, *Household Words*:

> I went to the Department of Practical Art in Marlborough House, to look over the museum of ornamental art. I had heard of a Chamber of Horrors there established, and I found it, and went through it with my catalogue. It was a gloomy chamber, hung round with frightful objects, in curtains, carpets, clothes, lamps, and what not. In each case the catalogue told me why such and such a thing wasn't endurable; and I found in the same place also, on equally good authority, in black and white, a few hints of what the correct principles of decoration are in each class of ornamental art. I could have cried, sir. I was ashamed of the pattern of my own trowsers, for I saw a piece of them hung up there as a horror. . . . I saw it all; when I went home I found that I had been living among horrors up to that hour.[22]

Henry Cole and those in his circle embodied the practical side of design reform in nineteenth-century England; they strove to bring responsibility to design by changing industry from within, anticipating that the involvement of artists as designers would bring about improvements in manufacture based on principles of fitness and restraint in ornamentation, and that through economical pricing, well-designed machine-made products would be available to the entire population. Their contemporary John Ruskin, the century's preeminent critic of art and architecture, did not consider fitness as

10 RICHARD REDGRAVE "Well Spring" jug, 1847. Made by J. F. Christy, Lambeth, England. Glass with painted and gilded decoration. Height 11″ (27.9 cm). Philadelphia Museum of Art. Purchased with funds given in memory of Sophie E. Pennebaker.

belonging to the physical aspects of an object and its function but a matter of the social and moral circumstances of its production. Instead of seeking to reform industry by argument and example, as Cole had tried to do, Ruskin called into question industrialization itself, setting forth his articles of faith in "The Nature of Gothic," published as part of *The Stones of Venice* (1853):

> We have much studied and much perfected, of late, the great civilized invention of the division of labour; only we give it a false name. It is not, truly speaking, the labour that is divided; but the men:— Divided into mere segments of men—broken into small fragments and crumbs of life; so that all the little piece of intelligence that is left in a man is not enough to make a pin, or a nail.... The great cry that rises from all our manufacturing cities, louder than their furnace blast, is all in very deed for this,—that we manufacture everything there except men; we blanch cotton, and strengthen steel, and refine sugar, and shape pottery; but to brighten, to strengthen, to refine, or to form a single living spirit, never enters into our estimate of advantages. And all the evil to which that cry is urging our myriads can be met only in one way ... by a right understanding, on the part of all classes, of what kinds of labour are good for men, raising them, and making them happy; by a determined sacrifice of such convenience, or beauty, or cheapness as is to be got only by the degradation of the workman; and by equally determined demand for the products and results of healthy and ennobling labour.[23]

Ruskin recognized "the individual value of every soul"[24] and the validity of the work of every man; like Pugin before him, he chose the Gothic as a preferred style because of its moral basis and its spirituality, and he championed a process of creation in which individual expression was supreme, even if products made by the workers' hands did not attain the high standards of finish that had been the goal of design since the Renaissance, and which the machine had now brought within the reach of everyone. Ruskin condemned precision for roughness, exact repetition for individuality, and prescription for expression, not coincidentally demoting the very qualities that could be best achieved by machine manufacture.

Following the social and moral values of Ruskin, William Morris, poet, socialist, painter, designer, and self-styled decorator, longed for the "day when millions of those who now sit in darkness will be enlightened by an art made by the people and for the people, a joy to the maker and the user."[25] Morris wanted to reinstitute a medieval approach to labor, to elevate the laborer with a craftsmanlike relation to his products, produced by hand in small, dedicated communities of skilled workers, furthering the aesthetic appreciation of Ruskin's principles of individuality and expression. Many of Morris's own designs were carried out in small workshops using the craft techniques of earlier times, which he and his workers had to devise afresh,

11 FORD MADDOX BROWN
Bedroom furniture in Kelmscott Manor, Oxfordshire, 1861–62. Made by Morris, Marshall, Faulkner and Company, London.

and through his hands-on experience, he honored the intrinsic qualities of his materials by knowing exactly what could be done with them.

Morris had turned to the design of utilitarian objects when he found that suitable pieces were not available for the furnishing of Red House in Kent, the home built for him in a new domestic vernacular style by Philip Webb in 1859, and he gathered a group of artists around him to help provide decoration for it. This led to the formation in 1861 of the decorating firm Morris, Marshall, Faulkner and Company as a type of artists' collaborative, with Morris as its mentor. Morris's taste itself was two-fold and seemingly contradictory: the company offered both simple, utilitarian furnishings based on English vernacular styles and such ornamental undertakings as gilded and painted furniture in a medieval style, whose elegance and elaboration Morris was able to justify for its symbolic value.[26] The poles of Morris production, whose common axis was their commitment to creativity and craftsmanship, could be defined by the spare "artisan's" furniture designed by the painter

Ford Maddox Brown (fig. 11) and the mahogany writing desk covered with foliage marquetry designed by George Washington Jack (fig. 12), as well as Morris's own densely patterned chintzes and wallpapers. A proponent of ornamentation that was adaptive—not imitative—of nature, Morris, like Redgrave, *The Journal of Design*, and others before him, espoused principles of ornamental fitness that sought to emphasize the flatness of surfaces by using all-over designs and by eschewing the three-dimensional effects and illusionism customary in decorative patterning at the time. Despite the promise of the firm's prospectus that "good decoration, involving rather the luxury of taste than the luxury of costliness, will be found to be much less expensive than is generally supposed,"[27] its products were costly because of the care paid to production and the intensiveness of the labor required to produce them, and far beyond the means of the "people" Morris had hoped to reach.

12 GEORGE WASHINGTON JACK
Secretaire cabinet, 1889. Made by Morris and Company, London. Mahogany with marquetry of various hardwoods. Height 51 1/2" (130.8 cm). Philadelphia Museum of Art. Gift of the Friends of the Philadelphia Museum of Art and gift (by exchange) of Julia G. Fahnestock in memory of William Fahnestock.

Morris's stated goal was to share the joy of the product as well as its production with the worker. Yet as the status of the craftsman grew, largely because of his efforts and those of the Arts and Crafts societies that followed his principles, his populist intent was negated by the cachet and thus the value that became attached to the aesthetics of handwork, as Thorstein Veblen described in his *Theory of the Leisure Class*:

> Hand labour is a more wasteful method of production; hence the goods turned out by this method are more serviceable for the purpose of pecuniary reputability; hence the marks of hand labour come to be honorific, and the goods which exhibit these marks take rank as of higher grade than the corresponding machine product.... Hence it comes about that the visible imperfections of the hand-wrought goods, being honorific, are accounted marks of superiority in point of beauty, or serviceability, or both. Hence has arisen that exaltation of the defective, of which John Ruskin and William Morris were such eager spokesmen in their time; and on this ground their propaganda of crudity and wasted effort has been taken up and carried forward since their time. And hence also the propaganda for a return to handicraft and household industry.[28]

In valuing handwork over industrial production, Morris preached a retrogressive and romantic utopianism, although as an employer he did not always live up to his own ideal of production by hand labor alone. His followers in the Arts and Crafts movement, whose work furthered the involvement of artists in the design of common objects, respected his principles more rigidly, promoting simplicity, honesty, and fitness; restraint in ornamentation; and a strict adherence to hand manufacture. Yet they were the link between English reformist design of the nineteenth century and Germany in the twentieth, where the development of industrial functionalism was to take place.

Notes

1 Xenophon, *Memorabilia*, III, viii, 6; translated by Anna S. Benjamin as *Recollections of Socrates and Socrates' Defense before the Jury* (Indianapolis: Bobbs-Merrill Company, 1965), p. 87. This passage from Xenophon was cited by Edward Robert De Zurko in *Origins of Functionalist Theory* (New York: Columbia University Press, 1957), p. 16.

2 *The Journal of Design* I (August 1849), p. 176.

3 See De Zurko, *Origins*, which traces the semantics of functionalism from antiquity to the mid-nineteenth century.

4 See Brent C. Brolin, *Flight of Fancy: The Banishment and Return of Ornament* (New York: St. Martin's Press, 1985), especially pp. 75–80.

5 A. W. N. Pugin, *Contrasts*, 2nd ed. [1841], repr. (New York: Humanities Press, 1969), p. 1.

6 See Ralph Lieberman, "The Crystal Palace," *AA Files*, no. 12 (Summer 1986), pp. 47–58; and Nikolaus Pevsner, *High Victorian Design: A Study of the Exhibits of 1851* (London: Architectural Press, 1951).

7 For example, Richard Redgrave, *Report on Design: Prepared as a Supplement to the Report of the Jury of Class XXX. of the Exhibition of 1851*, repr. (London: William Clowes and Sons, 1852); and Ralph Nicholson Wornum, "The Exhibition as a Lesson in Taste," in *The Art Journal Illustrated Catalogue: The Industry of All Nations 1851* (London: George Virtue, 1851), pp. 1–11***.

8 Redgrave, ibid., p. 3.

9 See Herwin Schaefer, *Nineteenth Century Modern: The Functional Tradition in Victorian Design* (New York and Washington, D. C.: Praeger Publishers, 1970).

10 Redgrave, *Report on Design*, p. 2.

11 First published in 1854; reprinted in Susan P. Casteras and Ronald Parkinson, eds., *Richard Redgrave, 1804–1888* (New Haven and London: Yale University Press in association with the Victoria and Albert Museum and the Yale Center for British Art, 1988), pp. 65–67.

12 "Address," *The Journal of Design* 1 (March 1849), p. 4.

13 Ibid., p. 5.

14 Ibid. (April 1849), p. 54.

15 See Elizabeth Bonython, *King Cole: A Picture Portrait of Sir Henry Cole, KCB, 1808–1882* (London: Victoria and Albert Museum, 1982); and *Fifty Years of Public Work of Sir Henry Cole, K. C. B., Accounted for in His Deeds, Speeches and Writings*, 2 vols. (London: George Bell and Sons, 1884).

16 According to a Society of Arts memorandum, published in Cole, *Fifty Years*, vol. 2, pp. 178–79.

17 Henry Cole, in ibid., vol. 1, p. 103 n. 1.

18 Reprinted in ibid., p. 108; see also Shirley Bury, "Felix Summerly's Art Manufactures," *Apollo* 85, n. s. (January 1967), pp. 28–33.

19 As for a cellaret designed by John Bell; see *The Journal of Design* 1 (June 1849), p. 111.

20 See ibid., vol. 1 (April 1849), pp. 33–34. "As a 'concetto,'" the *Journal* wrote, "it may be regarded as passable," but some of its elements were described as "ill-proportioned," and "in unity of detail and purpose it is somewhat defective."

21 Henry Cole, in *Fifty Years*, vol. 1, p. 285.

22 [Henry Morley], "A House Full of Horrors," *Household Words* 141 (December 4, 1852), pp. 265–66.

23 John Ruskin, "The Nature of Gothic," in *The Stones of Venice*, vol. 2 (London: Smith, Eden and Company, 1853), p. 165.

24 Ibid., p. 159.

25 William Morris, "The Beauty of Life," in G. D. H. Cole, ed., *William Morris* (London: Nonesuch Press, 1948), p. 564.

26 By accepting it as "state-furniture" in contrast to "necessary workaday furniture"; see Gillian Naylor, *The Arts and Crafts Movement. A Study of Its Sources, Ideals and Influences on Design Theory* (London: Studio Vista, 1971), p. 107.

27 Morris, Marshall, Faulkner and Company, prospectus, April 1861; reprinted in Ray Watkinson, *William Morris as Designer* (London: Studio Vista, 1967), p. 17.

28 Thorstein Veblen, *The Theory of the Leisure Class: An Economic Study of Institutions* [1899] (New York: The Modern Library, 1934), pp. 159, 161–62.

Absence of Ornament

A plain piece of furniture is more beautiful
than all the inlaid and carved museum pieces.

Adolf Loos[1]

If the nineteenth century disputed the appropriateness of ornament, the twentieth century resolved the issue by abandoning it altogether. The locus of this development was Germany and Austria, where it was promoted by various organizations working for the reform of design in industry. Its most strident spokesman was the Viennese architect Adolf Loos, who claimed that "the evolution of culture is synonymous with the removal of ornament from objects of daily use"[2] and whose own work was conceived in broad forms with

13 ADOLF LOOS
Armoire, c. 1901–2. Probably made by Friedrich Otto Schmidt, Vienna. Maple and brass. Height 78¾″ (200 cm). Musée d'Orsay, Paris.

7. Jahrgang
Luxus-Ausgabe
Nummer 15

SIMPLICISSIMUS

Illustrierte Wochenschrift

Deutsche im Ausland

So sahen Herr und Frau Schmidt aus, als sie nach London reisten, um sich die Krönung anzusehen.

Und so sahen sie aus, als sie nach acht Tagen als Mr. and Mrs. Smith zurückkehrten.

14 Cover of *Simplicissimus* (1902), with cartoon by Thomas Theodor Heine entitled "Germans Abroad": "This is how Herr and Frau Schmidt look when they travel to London to see the coronation, and this is how they look when they return after a week as Mr. and Mrs. Smith."

a minimum of applied decoration (fig. 13). "What makes our period so important," he wrote in his essay "Ornament and Crime," is that "we have outgrown ornament"; it is "no longer the expression of our culture." Looking back to a long history of artistic appreciation that had been biased toward ornamentation, he lamented the fact that "those objects without ornament, which mankind had created in earlier centuries, had been carelessly discarded and destroyed. We possess no carpenter's benches of the Carolingian period," he continued; "instead any rubbish which had even the smallest ornament was collected."[3]

The realization that design need no longer be dependent on ornament evolved from the example set in England at the end of the previous century, reflecting most directly the writings of John Ruskin and William Morris and the simple, solid, handcrafted products of the English Arts and Crafts

15 RICHARD RIEMERSCHMID Chair, 1898–99.
Made by the Vereinigte Werkstätten für Kunst im Handwerk, Munich.
Oak and leather. Height 30 5/8″ (77.8 cm).
Philadelphia Museum of Art. Purchased: Fiske Kimball Fund.

16 PETER BEHRENS
Glass service, 1898. Glass. Height of tallest glass 8 1/8″ (20.6 cm). Collection of Prof. Dr. Tilmann Buddensieg, Sinzig, Germany.

societies that were produced according to their principles.[4] These had a direct impact in Germany when they began to be included in exhibitions and imported for sale there, and through articles and illustrations in a number of newly founded English art journals that were widely read abroad, most notably *The Studio*. The English ideal was also interpreted by native critics such as Hermann Muthesius, a German envoy sent to London to study developments in English architecture and design, whose book *The English House*,[5] with its significant emphasis on Morris's contribution to interior design, had an especially strong influence. The result of this was an "artistic Anglomania"[6] in which everything in the simple and vernacular English style, from houses to carpentry to clothing, came to be preferred by those Germans with a progressive bent[7] (fig.14).

Unornamented simplicity in artistic manufactures had begun to receive praise in Germany at the end of the nineteenth century, particularly in reviews of the annual exhibitions of the fine and decorative arts. Richard Riemerschmid, the central figure in the Jugendstil movement in Munich, was lauded in 1899 as one of those artists who "aim to design plain and practical furniture for the middle class at reasonable prices and in good taste, like the English"[8] (fig. 15). The painter turned designer Peter Behrens was also singled out for his completely unornamented service of glasses for the table (fig. 16), displayed in a dining-room ensemble at the Munich exhibition of 1899, which the critic Julius Meier-Graefe noted were "calm and simple in their form, a conceit that one more and more comes to appreciate."[9] Like

Redgrave half a century earlier, Meier-Graefe seems to have been distinguishing works produced by artists and designers and shown in the context of exhibitions from objects of similar characteristics that had been available for decades, such as the serviceable glass used all over Germany in restaurants and the elegant, undecorated, commercially produced crystal available from even the finest glass houses, among them the Viennese manufacturer Lobmeyr (fig. 17).

A number of societies of artists, craftsmen, and manufacturers were established in Germany about this time following the aesthetics of William Morris, although they did not generally participate in his utopian, socialist ideal of

17 LUDWIG LOBMEYR
Carafe, c. 1856–76. Made by J & L Lobmeyr, Vienna. Glass. Height 11 13/16" (30 cm). Die Neue Sammlung, Munich.

the brotherhood of craftsmen; they were also too practical economically to support his rejection of machine manufacture. Rather they were dedicated to bringing artistic values to industry through the control of product design by artists, be it for handwork or machine production.[10] The Deutscher Werkbund (German Work Confederation), an umbrella association of artists, manufacturers, and design workshops founded in 1907 with the goal of promoting quality in German industry, is the organization that has most consistently been connected with the rejection of ornament and the introduction of a modern style that eventually came to be associated with the aesthetics of industrial production. There was, however, no philosophic or stylistic unanimity among its members. The multiplicity of their viewpoints was documented in the articles and illustrations published in its yearbooks between 1912 and 1915 and demonstrated in the exhibition that the Werkbund organized in Cologne in 1914 to celebrate its coming of age. While plates in the yearbooks have typically been cited by those who want to demonstrate the progressive leaning of the Werkbund—with examples in an unornamented style, such as the industrial architecture of Peter Behrens, the metalwork of Richard Riemerschmid, the Stuttgart designer Arthur Berger, and the Heilbronn

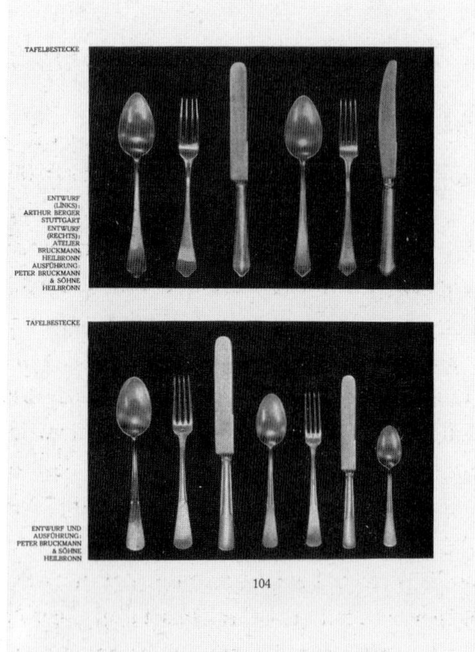
TAFELBESTECKE

ENTWURF (LINKS): ARTHUR BERGER STUTTGART ENTWURF (RECHTS): ATELIER BRUCKMANN HEILBRONN AUSFÜHRUNG: PETER BRUCKMANN & SÖHNE HEILBRONN

TAFELBESTECKE

ENTWURF UND AUSFÜHRUNG: PETER BRUCKMANN & SÖHNE HEILBRONN

104

TEEGESCHIRR

ENTWURF: RICHARD RIEMERSCHMID AUSFÜHRUNG: DEUTSCHE WERKSTÄTTEN A.-G. HELLERAU BEI DRESDEN

KAFFEEKANNE

ENTWURF: RICHARD RIEMERSCHMID MÜNCHEN AUSFÜHRUNG: DEUTSCHE WERKSTÄTTEN A.-G. HELLERAU BEI DRESDEN

105

18 Metalwork designed by Arthur Berger, Stuttgart, and Peter Bruckmann & Söhne, Heilbronn (left); and Richard Riemerschmid for the Deutsche Werkstätten, Hellerau (Dresden) (right). From *Jahrbuch des Deutschen Werkbundes* (1914).

19 LUCIAN BERNHARD
Bedroom shown at the Deutscher Werkbund exhibition in Cologne, 1914. From *Jahrbuch des Deutschen Werkbundes* (1915).

firm of Peter Bruckmann & Söhne (fig. 18)—they could as easily be used to show the conservatism and historicism of some of its members, as seen in the buildings of the Viennese master Josef Hoffmann in a neoclassical style and the tufted Empire bedroom interior by Lucian Bernhard of Berlin (better known as a brilliant poster designer), which were part of the Cologne exhibition (fig. 19).

The Werkbund did not come together under even a common thematic banner until after World War I, when its Württemberg chapter organized the exhibition "Die Form" in Stuttgart in the summer of 1924. The show included "only those objects from the realm of the applied arts which bear no ornament whatsoever ... [to] demonstrate the extraordinary wealth of expression that can be embodied in pure form without the addition of any ornament."[11] As early as 1907 Peter Behrens had emphasized the importance of form when he called for "a manner of design [to be] established appropriate to machine production. This will not be achieved through the imitation of handcraftsmanship, of other materials and of historical styles, but will be achieved through the most intimate union possible between art and industry. This could be done by concentrating on and implementing exactly the technique of mechanical production in order to arrive by artistic means at those forms that derive directly from and correspond to the machine and machine production.... The attempt should now be made, using standard types, to achieve a graceful beauty that is cleanly constructed and appropriate to the materials used."[12]

Hermann Muthesius had underscored the importance of considering form as the singular contribution of the designer when he insisted in 1913 that even industrial objects must "be regarded from the point of view of form, i.e., the effect they will have on the eye.... The idea that it is quite sufficient for the engineer designing a building, an appliance, a machine, merely to fulfil a purpose, is erroneous, and the recent often-repeated suggestion that if the object fulfils its purpose then it is beautiful as well is even more erroneous. Usefulness has basically nothing to do with beauty. Beauty is a problem of form, and nothing else."[13] The importance to be given to form was also emphasized by Walter Gropius in 1916—if only as a matter of practicality in distinguishing one's own products from one's competitors'—in his recommendations supporting the concept of a design school that would supply advice and models for industry: "In the entire field of trade and industry," he wrote, "there has arisen a demand for beauty of external form as well as for technical and economic perfection. Apparently, material improvement of products

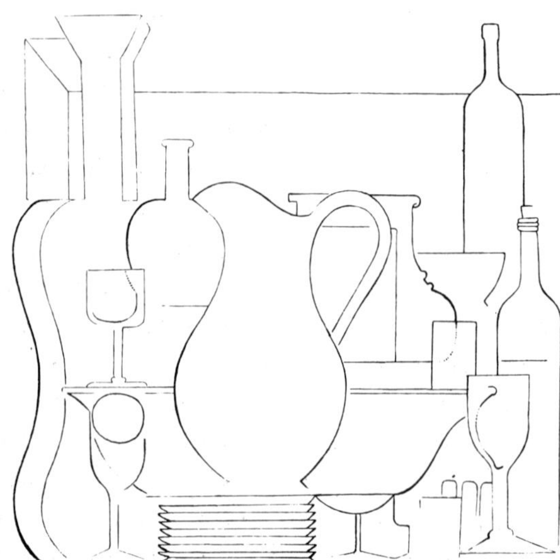

20 AMÉDÉE OZENFANT AND LE CORBUSIER
Composition. From *La Peinture moderne* (Paris, n.d.). Musée des Arts Décoratifs, Paris, Library.

21 RICHARD HERRE
Poster for the Deutscher Werkbund exhibition "Die Form," Stuttgart, 1924.

does not by itself suffice to achieve victories in international competitions. A thing that is technically excellent in all respects must be impregnated with an intellectual idea—with form—in order to secure preference among the large quantity of products of the same kind."[14] Gropius intellectualized form by equating it with geometry: "The basic building elements—throughout time and in all countries—consist of the geometric trilogy ensuring validity in all human creativity."[15] The square, circle, and triangle, the cube, sphere, and pyramid—these were also at the heart of the philosophy and teachings of Wassily Kandinsky, Paul Klee, and Johannes Itten, masters who taught at the Bauhaus design school in Weimar under Gropius.

Geometry's perfection also influenced thinkers elsewhere. In the Netherlands the De Stijl designer Theo van Doesburg saw it as the basis for a new machine style, "for only the machine can produce this constructive precision. The new possibilities created by the machine resulted in an up-to-date aesthetic."[16] This machine aesthetic, based on geometry, found its fullest expres-

48

Samowar
Entwurf und Ausführung
Ernſt Lichtblau
Wien

Mokkamaſchine
Entwurf und Ausführung
Staatliches Bauhaus
Weimar

Die Form I. 4

49

Meſſingkanne
Entwurf Ferdinand Kramer
Ausführung Emil Graf
Frankfurt a. M.

Meſſingkanne
Entwurf und Ausführung
Staatliches Bauhaus
Weimar

sion in France, in the writings of Le Corbusier, who described a "beauty based on purity of form and precise execution. Machines are replacing hand work; the spheres are smooth; the cylinders have the kind of precision only attainable in theory: without fuss, the machine produces surfaces which are faultless."[17] Precise, faultless, smooth forms were depicted by Le Corbusier and Amédée Ozenfant, leaders of the Purist movement, in their drawn and painted compositions of standardized and repeated objects of everyday use (fig. 20), which they conceived as generated by a "*law of mechanical selection.* This established that objects tend toward a type that is determined by the evolution of forms between the ideal of the greatest utility and that which satisfies the necessities of economic production."[18]

The poster Richard Herre designed for the Werkbund exhibition "Die Form" (fig. 21), with its regularized commercial furnishings, ceramic vessels in graduated sizes, and marquee-style block lettering, implied that this was a presentation of such industrial forms—geometric, anonymous, and repetitive. While several of the 173 plates in the catalogue, *Form ohne Ornament* (Form without Ornament),[19] do illustrate industrial products such as chemists' flasks, electrical machinery, and door handles, the majority of the objects—including furniture, metalwork (fig. 22), glassware (fig. 23), ceramics (fig. 24), and lighting—were individualistic, expressive, and obviously handmade, demonstrating that the absence of ornament and reliance on form alone did not yield any one aesthetic, and not in the least an industrial one. The items illustrated in the plates devoted to the Bauhaus were no more technological in their appearance than the others, and considering today's image of the school's creations as unique in their time, they blend surprisingly smoothly with the other objects illustrated (fig. 22). The only distinctive characteristic of the Bauhaus illustrations is that the names of the individual designers are not given, reflecting the image the school wanted to project of being a collective (although many objects were fully identified by designer in concurrent publications of the Bauhaus itself).

A new emphasis on the production aesthetics of collectivity and anonymity had emerged at the Bauhaus in 1923, when the direction of its activity shifted from its founding call for a "return to the crafts" and its creation as "a new guild of craftsmen"[20] to the application of handcraftsmanship to the production of prototypes for industry. The change in the school's philosophy is mirrored in two different versions of a tea infuser created in 1924 by Marianne Brandt, the only woman member of the Bauhaus metal workshop. On first view, the two versions of the teapot, a study in the relationship of geometric forms, seem almost identical. But one, made of silver (colorplate 1), clearly reveals its handcrafted nature in the repeated marks of the hammer that cover the surface of its spherical bowl, witness to the arduous process of

22 Metalwork designed by Ernst Lichtblau (top left), Ferdinand Kramer (bottom left), and at the Bauhaus, Weimar, by Wilhelm Wagenfeld (top right) and Martin Jahn (bottom right). From *Die Form ohne Ornament* (Stuttgart, 1925). Philadelphia Museum of Art Library.

23 Glassware designed by Elfe Wenz-Vietor. From *Die Form ohne Ornament* (Stuttgart, 1925). Philadelphia Museum of Art Library.

its creation. The second, of brass (colorplate 2), takes the same shape, but its bowl is smooth and reflective, masking all evidence of its hand manufacture under a highly finished surface, implying that it could have been made by machine.

Other designers were also beginning to reject the marks of personal expression and handwork in favor of a detached, anonymous look. At the Handwerker- und Kunstgewerbeschule at Burg Giebichenstein in Halle, Gustav Weidanz chose smooth and simple shapes for his somewhat futuristic ceramic tea service (fig. 25),[21] while the flat, angular cutlery produced in Berlin by the

24 Ceramic pitcher designed by Herta Bucher. From *Die Form ohne Ornament* (Stuttgart, 1925). Philadelphia Museum of Art Library.

25 GUSTAV WEIDANZ
Teapots, 1922–23. Made at the Burg Giebichenstein ceramic workshop, Halle/Saale. Glazed earthenware. Burg Giebichenstein, Halle/Saale.

young silversmith Andreas Moritz (fig. 26) and the pitcher with an elegant (albeit exaggerated) silhouette designed by the Danish architect Kay Fisker (fig. 27) share an emphasis on unbroken and unadorned reflective surfaces and a precision then associated with machine manufacture rather than the handcraftsmanship by which they were made. The table lamp created by Karl J. Jucker and Wilhelm Wagenfeld from cylinder and sphere (colorplate 3) was also suggestive of this notion of machine perfection; made by hand in the Bauhaus workshops, it combined basic forms fabricated from industrial materials. Wagenfeld recalled how "dealers and manufacturers laughed over our products" when they were displayed at a trade fair in Leipzig. "Although they looked like cheap machine products, they were in fact expensive handicrafts."[22] This was a reversal of the paradox of honorific valuation described by Thorstein Veblen in 1899: the earlier preference for the obviously handmade was now replaced with a preference for the apparently machine made, yielding what might be called, in a variation of Veblen's term, an exaltation of the "perfective." At last, the perfect finish that could be achieved by machine was valued—but for items produced in such small numbers as these, the perfection of the machine had to be simulated by hand.

During the late 1920s and 1930s, several large German manufacturers of decorative ceramics, glassware, and metalware took steps to bring some of their products in line with these new concepts of spare design by removing both molded and applied ornament from them. A number of designers associated with the Staatliche Porzellan-Manufaktur in Berlin, including Trude Petri and Marguerite Friedländer, modernized the factory's wares with services conceived for manufacture in white porcelain with smooth shapes and surfaces designed for efficient production (although they could also be bought with restrained painted decorations), while Hermann Gretsch capitalized on this same aesthetic at the Arzberg porcelain factory. Advertising and promotion followed this new direction: Friedländer's porcelain service was photographed stacked as if just out of the kiln, signifying standardized mass production (fig. 28), and Lily Reich installed an exhibition of ceramics using the same idea, alluding to the possibility of endless production runs (fig. 29). The Jenaer glassworks, which had exhibited glass laboratory jars and ovenproof casseroles in "Die Form" in 1924, produced a heat-

26 ANDREAS MORITZ
Cutlery, c. 1925. Silver. Length of knife 9½" (24 cm). Kunstgewerbemuseum, Berlin. Gift of the artist.

27 KAY FISKER Pitcher, 1927.
Made by A. Michelsen, Copenhagen. Silver. Height 10 7/16" (26.5 cm).
Philadelphia Museum of Art. Gift of Mrs. Albert M. Greenfield.

28 MARGUERITE FRIEDLÄNDER
Coffee service, 1930.
Made by the Staatliche Porzellan-Manufaktur, Berlin.
From *Form* (February 15, 1930).

29 LILY REICH
"Bright Earth, Fired Earth," installation at the "Deutsches Volk – Deutsche Arbeit" exhibition, Berlin, 1934.

30 WILHELM WAGENFELD
"Kubus" food-storage containers, 1938. Made by Vereinigte Lausitzer Glaswerke AG, Weisswasser, Germany. Large dish 3 1/2 x 7 1/8 x 7 1/8" (9 x 18 x 18 cm). Die Neue Sammlung, Munich.

resistant glass tea set designed by Wilhelm Wagenfeld in 1931 that was based on such precedents (fig. 31); in the United States, the inventor Peter Schlumbohm, continuing work he had begun in Germany, also relied on the concept of laboratory glassware for the domestic utensils he created for his "Chemist's Kitchen," borrowing laboratory procedures such as filtration for their functions as well (fig. 32). Wagenfeld, who in 1935 became artistic director of the Lausitzer glassworks, designed a set of compact cubic containers based on a modular system that stacked into a unit for efficient storage (fig. 30), which in spite of their obvious industrial inspiration were promoted as perfectly adapted for table use. Wagenfeld continued to be a spokesman for collective and anonymous design. He had advised against having his name associated with the tea service he designed for Jenaer, for he felt that the emphasis of advertising and promotion should remain with the product itself. "This," he stated, "is perhaps the main difference between handcraft and industry. The former is still bound to the individual ... whereas the industrial product is the expression of collective work and collective execution. Only through the joint efforts of designer, technician, and craftsman does the [industrial] product arrive at its final form."[23]

32 Brochure for Peter Schlumbohm's "Chemex" coffeemaker, 1941, Chemex Corporation (1948). Philadelphia Museum of Art.

31 WILHELM WAGENFELD Tea service, 1931. Made by Jenaer Glaswerk, Schott & Gen., Jena, Germany. Glass. Height of teapot 4½" (11.5 cm). Die Neue Sammlung, Munich.

Notes

1 Adolf Loos, "Ornament and Crime" [1908]; translated in Arts Council of Great Britain, *The Architecture of Adolf Loos* (n.p., 1985), p. 100.

2 Ibid.

3 Ibid, pp. 100, 102.

4 These included the Century Guild, established by Arthur Heygate Macmurdo in 1882; the Art-Workers Guild, organized in 1884; and the School and Guild of Handicraft, founded by Charles Robert Ashbee in 1888.

5 Hermann Muthesius, *Das Englische Haus*, 3 vols. (Berlin: E. Wasmuth, 1904–5); see the abridged translation edited by Dennis Sharp, *The English House* (New York: Rizzoli, 1987).

6 Richard Graul, "Deutschland," in Richard Graul, ed., *Die Krisis im Kunstgewerbe* (Leipzig, 1901), p. 40; quoted in Kathryn B. Hiesinger, ed., *Art Nouveau in Munich: Masters of Jugendstil* (Philadelphia: Philadelphia Museum of Art in association with Prestel, 1988), p. 17.

7 Loos, for example, was a contributor to this; see his essays praising aspects of English style and manufacture in Adolf Loos, *Spoken into the Void: Collected Essays 1897–1900* (Cambridge, Mass., and London: The MIT Press, 1982).

8 Georg Fuchs, "Angewandte Kunst im Glaspalaste 1898," *Deutsche Kunst und Dekoration* 5 (1899–1900), p. 34; quoted in Hiesinger, *Art Nouveau*, p. 17.

9 Julius Meier-Graefe, "Peter Behrens," *Dekorative Kunst* 5 (1900), p. 3. Translations are the author's unless otherwise noted.

10 See John Heskett, *German Design, 1870–1918* (New York: Taplinger Publishing Company, 1986), pp. 93–105.

11 "Invitation to Participate in the Werkbund Exhibition *Die Form*"; quoted in Karin Kirsch, *The Weissenhofsiedlung: Experimental Housing Built for the Deutscher Werkbund, Stuttgart, 1927* (New York: Rizzoli, 1989), p. 11.

12 Peter Behrens, *Berliner Tageblatt*, August 29, 1907; translated as "Art in Technology," in Tilmann Buddensieg, *Industriekultur: Peter Behrens and the AEG, 1907–1914* (Cambridge, Mass., and London: The MIT Press, 1984), p. 208.

13 Hermann Muthesius, "Das Formenproblem im Ingenieurbau," *Jahrbuch des Deutschen Werkbundes* (Jena, 1913); translated as "The Problem of Form in Engineering," in Tim Benton and Charlotte Benton, with Dennis Sharp, eds., *Form and Function. A Source Book for the History of Architecture and Design 1890–1939* (London: Crosby Lockwood Staples in association with the Open University Press, 1975), pp. 116, 117.

14 Walter Gropius, "Recommendations for the Founding of an Educational Institution as an Artistic Counseling Service for Industry, the Trades, and the Crafts" [1916]; translated in Hans M. Wingler, *The Bauhaus: Weimar Dessau Berlin Chicago* (Cambridge, Mass., and London: The MIT Press, 1969), p. 23

15 Walter Gropius [1923], quoted in Württembergischer Kunstverein, Stuttgart, *50 Years Bauhaus* (1968), p. 21.

16 Theo van Doesburg, "The Will to Style," *De Stijl* 5 (February–March 1922); translated in Joost Baljeu, *Theo van Doesburg* (New York: Macmillan Publishing Company, 1974), p. 122.

17 Le Corbusier, "Construire en série" [1924], in *Almanach d'architecture moderne* (Paris: Les Éditions G. Crès et Cie., 1925), pp. 76–77; translated as "Mass Produced Buildings," in Benton, Benton, and Sharp, eds., *Form and Function*, p. 134.

18 Amédée Ozenfant and Charles-Edouard Jeanneret [Le Corbusier], *La Peinture moderne* (Paris: Les Éditions G. Crès et Cie., n. d.), p. 167.

19 *Die Form ohne Ornament: Werkbundausstellung 1924* (Stuttgart, Berlin, and Leipzig: Deutsche Verlags-Anstalt, 1925).

20 Walter Gropius, *Programm des Staatlichen Bauhauses in Weimar* (Weimar: Staatliche Bauhaus, 1919); translated as "Program of the Staatliche Bauhaus in Weimar," in Wingler, *The Bauhaus*, p. 31.

21 For an overview of the school at Burg Giebichenstein, see Renate Luckner-Bien, "Burg und Bauhaus," in Museum für Gestaltung, Zurich, *Bauhaus 1919–1933* (1988), pp. 45–53.

22 Wilhelm Wagenfeld, quoted in Magdalena Droste, *Bauhaus, 1919–1933* (Cologne: Benedikt Taschen, 1993), p. 80.

23 Wilhelm Wagenfeld, "Jenaer Glas," *Schaulade* (1932), p. 199; translated in Kathryn B. Hiesinger and George H. Marcus, *Landmarks of Twentieth-Century Design* (New York: Abbeville Press, 1993), p. 128.

Standardization

Standard needs, standard functions,
hence standard objects, standard furniture.

Le Corbusier [1]

The first comprehensive public expression of functionalism appeared in 1927 at the Deutscher Werkbund exhibition in Stuttgart entitled "Die Wohnung" (The Dwelling). In its presentation of model housing and modern household furnishings the association came together behind a single, forward-looking goal.[2] This was reinforced visually in three posters created for "Die Wohnung." Two, designed by Willi Baumeister, showed heavily furnished, ornate, and old-fashioned interiors slashed over with large red X's (fig. 33); the third, a photomontage by Karl Straub, showed the modern structures, spare interiors, and manufactured objects that were part of the exhibition (fig. 34).

"Die Wohnung" was in two parts, a new housing development built on a hillside in the Weissenhof section of Stuttgart (a model of which is seen in Straub's poster), and a complementary presentation of materials, products, and furnishings in an exhibition hall in the center of the city. In charge of the exhibition as artistic director was Ludwig Mies van der Rohe, activist architect from Berlin and deputy chairman of the Werkbund; he also created the site plan for the development and designed its largest structure, a four-story building with twenty-four apartments. Weissenhof was a truly international undertaking, and although Mies did not have complete control over the selection of architects, he was able to involve a number of the most progressive designers then practicing in Europe, including Le Corbusier, Walter Gropius, and the Dutchman J. J. P. Oud. The development's twenty-one apartment buildings, row houses, and detached single-family dwellings—structures made of reinforced concrete with flat roofs and horizontal strip windows—demonstrated with a surprising overall unity the international character of the new architectural style.

In agreeing to fund the Werkbund exhibition, the city council of Stuttgart had hoped to include Weissenhof as part of its program of mass housing for the working classes, but as the project developed the earlier plan for inexpensive, standardized, mass-produced buildings was transformed into a more costly development of prototypes for modern housing and a showplace for new construction techniques and materials. Rationalization and standardization of production, which was one of the rationales for "Die Wohnung" and

33 WILLI BAUMEISTER
Poster for the Deutscher Werkbund exhibition "Die Wohnung," Stuttgart, 1927.

which Mies had acknowledged was demanded by "economic considerations today,"[3] was more fully realized in the interiors, many of them open-plan schemes with simple, logical, and utilitarian furnishings. The buildings were furnished by the development's seventeen architects along with thirty-eight other designers—mostly from Germany, and particularly Stuttgart, where a number had connections to the Kunstgewerbeschule; and from Austria as well as a collective from the Schweizer (Swiss) Werkbund. Although the stylistic unity of the structures was not brought inside, the interiors were generally simple and unornamented, and shared a preference for modular and component furniture systems of wood, plywood, and metal and for rationalized lighting—standardized, mass produced, and inexpensive—reflecting the social goals of progressive design and the ideas of efficiency of manufacture introduced in Germany in the preceding decades.

Standardization and interchangeability of elements had become the hallmark of Germany's rapidly growing manufacturers of tools, equipment, and machinery following production practices introduced in similar industries in the later nineteenth century, especially in the United States.[4] The forms of their products were not necessarily different from those of indi-

34 KARL STRAUB
Poster for the Deutscher Werkbund exhibition "Die Wohnung," Stuttgart, 1927.

vidualized handmade goods nor particularly advanced, and had generally been determined along with their inner parts by engineers, not designers. A newsworthy change in this practice occurred in 1907 when the Allgemeine Elektricitäts-Gesellschaft (AEG), the mammoth manufacturer of electrical products, created the post of artistic adviser and hired an artist-designer, Peter Behrens, to fill it. Behrens put his mark on everything from switches, lamps, and appliances to catalogues, advertising, and the company's factory buildings; his work was a paradigm of the goal of the Deutscher Werkbund, founded the same year, which sought to bring quality to industry through the participation of artists and designers. Behrens took his involvement well beyond the outer skin of AEG products to work with the company's engineers on broad aspects of manufacturing, introducing a new, integrated approach to design.

Behrens contributed most to four major product lines—arc lamps, clocks, fans, and kettles—with his transformations resulting in subtle redesigns that cleaned up their forms and brought them within his idea of the company's overall design image. He introduced concepts of standardization, exploring them most fully in the kettles, which had electrical components in

ELEKTRISCHE TEE- UND WASSERKESSEL
NACH ENTWÜRFEN VON PROF. PETER BEHRENS

Messing glatt, matt
achteckige Form

PL Nr	Inhalt ca. l	Gewicht ca. kg	Preis Mk.
3588	0,75	1,75	20,–
3598	1,25	1,0	22,–
3608	1,75	1,1	24,–

Kupfer flockig gehämmert
achteckige Form

PL Nr	Inhalt ca. l	Gewicht ca. kg	Preis Mk.
3589	0,75	0,75	22,–
3599	1,25	1,0	24,–
3690	1,75	1,1	26,–

Messing vernickelt, glatt
achteckige Form

PL Nr	Inhalt ca. l	Gewicht ca. kg	Preis Mk.
3587	0,75	0,75	19,–
3597	1,25	1,0	22,–
3607	1,75	1,1	23,–

ALLGEMEINE ELEKTRICITÄTS-GESELLSCHAFT
ABT. HEIZAPPARATE

35 PETER BEHRENS
Electric tea and water kettles in three finishes, 1909. From Allgemeine Elektricitäts-Gesellschaft catalogue. Collection of Henning Rogge.

common and a number of interchangeable elements, such as lids, handles, and bases (fig. 35). The kettles were available in round, octagonal, and oval shapes, with smooth, grooved, and hammered finishes, in nickel-plated brass, matte brass, and copper, and although not all possible variations were available, some thirty different combinations of elements, materials, finishes, and shapes could be ordered. As much as Behrens wished to avoid imitating handcraftsmanship with machine manufacture, his success was only partial, for the company had to take into account the varied wishes of its market. Only the line with the smooth finish could be said to respond to Behrens's call for a "cleanly constructed" style related to the machine; the grooved and hammered finishes, although created by machine and "appropriate"[5] to the material, remained imitations of handcraftsmanship.

Standardized elements were also introduced into the German furniture industry, not just for the utilitarian lines such as office fittings but for what we might continue to call the art manufactures, the two most celebrated examples being the *Maschinenmöbel* (machine-made furniture) program of the Dresdner Werkstätten für Handwerkskunst (Dresden Workshops for Arts and Crafts) and the *Typenmöbel* (standardized furniture) program of the Vereinigte Werkstätten für Kunst im Handwerk (United Workshops for Art in Handicraft) in Munich. What was particularly significant about these endeavors was that standardization had become the domain of architects and designers hired by manufacturers to create modern lines of home furnishings, and that at least certain echelons of the public were comfortable enough with the status of machine-produced household goods that these terms could be used to identify and publicize their products (fig. 36). *Maschinenmöbel*, plain, angular, and unornamented furniture designed by Richard Riemerschmid for a reform-minded clientele and constructed by hand from machine-made elements, was sold in living room, kitchen, and bedroom ensembles at several price levels. It included components that could be stacked or joined side by side to form large case pieces, such as an oak buffet made up of three separate cupboard units (fig. 37). When this line was first exhibited in Dresden in 1906, the critic Ernst Zimmermann concluded in an article entitled "Artistic *Maschinenmöbel*" that "here, a problem of great significance has been seized with unusual energy and success and brought to a resolution that appears to be thoroughly practical."[6]

Typenmöbel, initiated in 1907 by Bruno Paul, a founding member at the Vereinigte Werkstätten, was rationalized for production to a much greater degree. Similarly manufactured in series with the use of machinery, and

36 Poster for the Vereinigte Werkstätten exhibition "Typenmöbel," 1908. Kunstbibliothek, Berlin.

forward-looking in its typological differentiation and unit conception, Paul's furniture aimed at a broader market and more varied taste levels than Riemerschmid's. While some of Paul's designs were plain, others featured inlaid ornamental patterns (fig. 38) and complicated, curved forms of laminated wood that were more costly to manufacture and used machines in a more sophisticated but less efficient manner. The *Typenmöbel* program, which never professed an aesthetic related to the machine—it was enough that furniture could be made at lower cost and sold more cheaply—flourished. By the time of the Werkbund exhibition in Cologne in 1914, the concept had expanded, and could accommodate the work of twenty designers as diverse in their stylistic preferences as Behrens, Adelbert Niemeyer, Josef Hoffmann, and Karl Bertsch (fig. 39). The success of the furniture was explained to the readers of "*The Studio*" *Yearbook of Decorative Art* as the happy result of "economic considerations":

> Their constituent parts are made in many different but definitely standardised sizes, shapes, and proportions, and admit of manifold combinations and varieties of shape; while the choice of numerous kinds of wood enables such variations to be made that, in spite of the definite limitation of sizes and proportions, there is practically no restraint on the exercise of artistic fantasy and formative skill. The great economic advantage of this mode of production arises from the fact that all these single parts, of which there are something like 800 different kinds, can be made in large quantities and with the most advantageous employment of machine labour; while the extensive range of combinations ensures to the complete article an individuality and character of its own, without betraying the use of machinery in its production.[7]

In emphasizing the individuality of expression and variety of styles that could be achieved within a program of standard components or types, the author was expressing one point of view in a famous controversy that occurred at the annual conference held during the 1914 Werkbund exhibition. The participants fell into two camps: those like the civil servant Hermann Muthesius, who, in the ten propositions he put forth in Cologne, spoke out for standardization, which would "alone make possible the development of universally valid, unfailing good taste"[8] on which he felt the future of German manufacturing was based, and those like the Belgian architect Henry van de Velde, who stood on the side of individuality and refused any suggestion that canons or norms be imposed on the artist for the sake of commercial success. Walter Gropius later wrote of "every form as the embodiment of an idea, every piece of work as a manifestation of our innermost selves,"[9] revealing his philosophy of individualistic design that formed the basis for the original program of the Bauhaus. The school made a complete about-face around 1923, when it adopted the slogan "art and technology, a new unity!"

37 RICHARD RIEMERSCHMID Buffet from *Maschinenmöbel* series, 1906. Made by the Werkstätten für Handwerkskunst, Dresden. Fumed oak and iron. Height 82¼″ (209 cm). Kunstgewerbemuseum, Dresden.

"The creation of standard types for all practical commodities of everyday use is a social necessity," Gropius wrote from this new perspective a few years later. "On the whole," he said, "the necessities of life are the same for the majority of people. The home and its furnishings are mass consumer goods, and their design is more a matter of reason than a matter of passion.... There is no danger that standardization will force a choice upon the individual, since due to natural competition the number of available types of each object will always be ample to provide the individual with a choice of design that suits him best."[10]

For Le Corbusier, the choice was already made. He rejected the idea that utilitarian objects should be given individualistic or creative forms by architects and designers: "All the humbug talked about the unique, the precious 'piece,' rings false and shows a pitiful lack of understanding of the needs of the present day: a chair is in no way a work of art; a chair has no soul; it is a machine for sitting in."[11] Le Corbusier favored standard equipment that had been created by engineers and was already on the market; "articles of perfect convenience and utility, that soothe our spirits with the luxury afforded

38 BRUNO PAUL
Sideboard from *Typenmöbel* series, 1911. Made by the Vereinigte Werkstätten für Kunst im Handwerk, Bremen.

39 KARL BERTSCH
Study shown at the Deutscher Werkbund exhibition in Cologne, 1914. From *"The Studio" Yearbook of Decorative Arts* (1914). Philadelphia Museum of Art Library.

by the elegance of their conception, the purity of their execution, and the efficiency of their operation,"[12] were ready to satisfy what he pointed out were shared, standard, human needs. Le Corbusier himself chose off-the-rack chairs and tables for his interiors, including his first major showcase, the Pavillon de l'Esprit Nouveau; designed with his associate and distant cousin Pierre Jeanneret, this structure was also built of standardized components and shown as an example of a typical modern living unit at the Exposition Internationale des Arts Décoratifs et Industriels Modernes in Paris in 1925. Clearly distinguishable in the photographs (fig. 40) are two of his favorite examples of standard furniture, a bentwood armchair manufactured in great numbers since the nineteenth century by the Viennese firm Gebrüder Thonet and an upholstered club chair of the kind made in England by Maple & Company.[13] These he saw as representative types that over years of manufacture had been refined for efficiency of production and optimum satisfaction of human physical and psychological needs.[14]

Le Corbusier's choice of lighting also relied on basic equipment. Like Gerrit Rietveld in the Netherlands, who as early as 1920 had created fixtures out of unshielded tubular light bulbs arranged in open constructions sus-

40 LE CORBUSIER AND PIERRE JEANNERET
Pavillon de l'Esprit Nouveau, Paris, 1925. Musée des Arts Décoratifs, Paris.

pended simply with electrical wire (fig. 41)—a conception Walter Gropius followed for his office at the Bauhaus in Weimar—Le Corbusier mounted exposed tubular bulbs as wall sconces in the Pavillon de l'Esprit Nouveau and in houses such as the one he designed for Raoul La Roche in Neuilly in 1923–25 (fig. 42). In his buildings at Weissenhof he suspended a bare bulb by an electric wire from the ceiling to illuminate a bedroom (fig. 44), while a simple glass globe hung in the center of a living area. A new field, electric lighting had adapted well to the use of stock industrial products and to mass production; changes in lighting design came about, as Gropius pointed out, "by resolute consideration of modern production methods, constructions, and materials," evolving forms "that often... deviate from the conventional."[15]

Fourteen examples of lighting fixtures were highlighted in *Innenräume*,[16] the Werkbund's volume of furnishings and interiors published in 1928 to

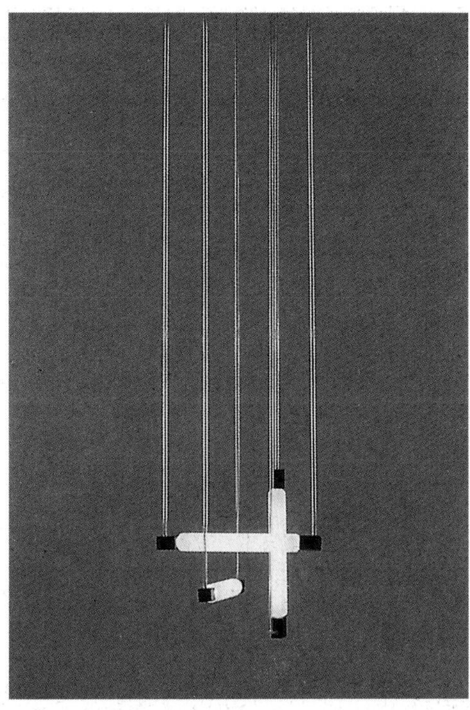

41 GERRIT RIETVELD
Hanging lamp, 1920. Reproduction made by Tecta, Lauenförde, Germany. Glass and wood. Length of each unit 15 3/4″ (40 cm).

42 LE CORBUSIER Wall lamp from the Villa La Roche, Paris, 1923–25. Metal and glass.

commemorate its "Die Wohnung" exhibition in Stuttgart. Made primarily of metal and glass, they were supplied by the few manufacturers internationally who were then producing lighting in a modern style. These included three variants from the "PH" series designed by Poul Henningsen, an architect from Copenhagen, who had won a gold medal for their prototypes at the Paris exposition of 1925 (fig. 43). Manufactured by the Danish firm of Louis Poulsen (and still in production), they improved on generalized room lighting because the form and position of the shades had been carefully considered to control the amount and direction of the light. Among the others were an impressive nickeled-steel floor lamp by Richard Döcker of Stuttgart (fig. 45) and a wall-mounted fixture with a glass globe on a swivel arm made of the alloy electrum, designed by Max Ernst Haefeli (also still in production) and used in the Schweizer Werkbund's collectively furnished interiors. Hanging fixtures by

Left:
43 POUL HENNINGSEN
Hanging lamp, 1926. Made by Louis Poulsen & Company, Copenhagen. Opal glass and brass. Diameter 19⅝″ (50 cm). Louis Poulsen & Company, Copenhagen.

Below:
44 LE CORBUSIER
House at Weissenhofsiedlung, Stuttgart, 1927, with tubular metal beds designed by Alfred Roth, Thonet bentwood chairs, and bare light bulb. Staatliches Hochbauamt, Stuttgart.

Adolf Meyer, who had been a partner of Gropius, produced by Zeiss-Ikon-Werke of Berlin; by Marianne Brandt (one, which was adjustable, designed with Hans Przyrembel) and by the Dutch firm Gispen (fig. 47) were also represented. Brandt's collaboration with industry continued to grow in the next years, when she produced among other designs the "Bauhaus Model" ceiling-mounted fixtures for Schwintzer & Greff of Berlin, and a line of basic bedside lamps designed with Hin Brendendieck for Körting & Matthieson in Leipzig (fig. 46).

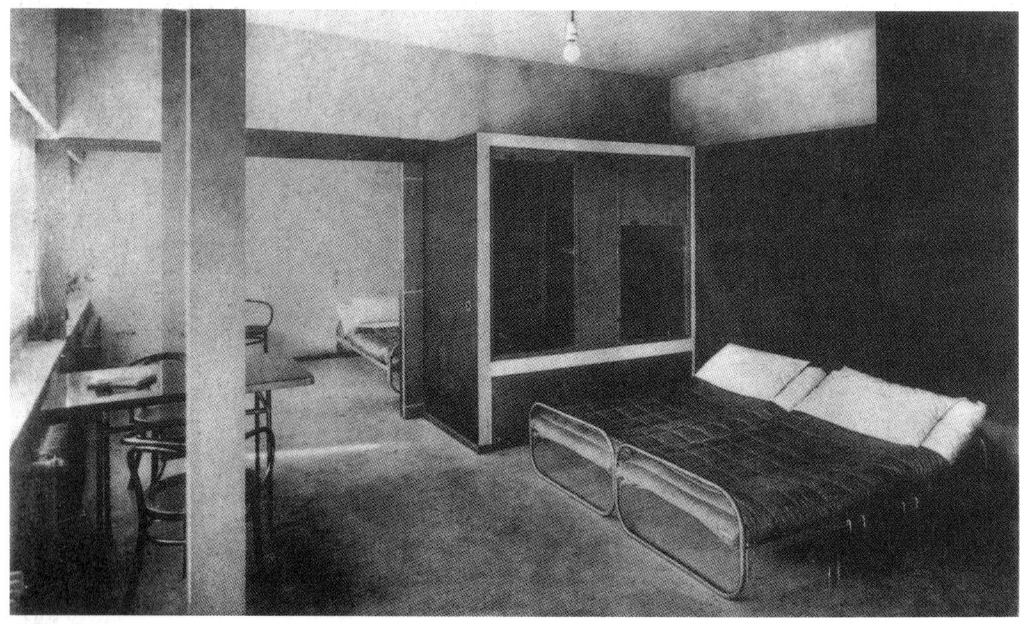

Mies van der Rohe's instructions for furnishing Weissenhof with modern interiors had told the architects and designers to maintain the "character" of the buildings and avoid "everything pretentiously bourgeois and superfluous."[17] For seating, many used pieces already in production (notably the bentwood chairs manufactured by Thonet with industrial procedures and knocked down for efficient shipping), and they favored other standardized furniture types as well, some already available and others designed especially for the exhibition. These ranged widely in their level of sophistication and their style, encompassing modular storage systems; wooden furniture, some severely rationalized but most generally related to vernacular types in the Arts and Crafts tradition; and metal chairs and tables. The number and variety of examples shown at Weissenhof alone suggest the extent of consideration that had already been given to component and modular furnishing during the 1920s.

In Stuttgart as in Paris, Le Corbusier found nothing commercial that was suitable for use as storage furniture, what he called "the problem of the cabinets [*casiers*]."[18] Forced to develop his own, he devised an impersonal, astylistic system based on a module of seventy-five centimeters, which he derived from a simple investigation of everyday needs:

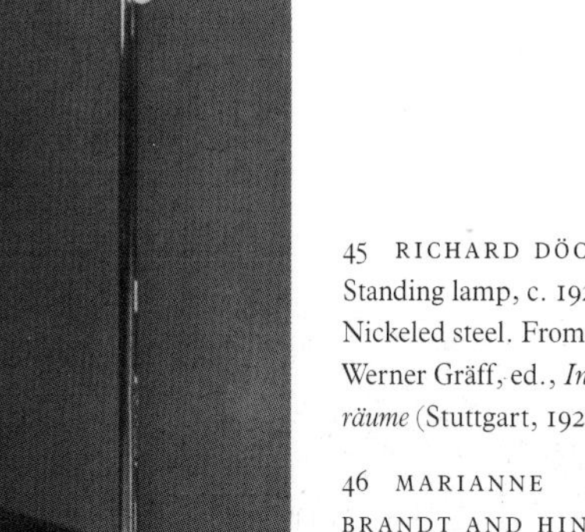

45 RICHARD DÖCKER
Standing lamp, c. 1927. Nickeled steel. From Werner Gräff, ed., *Innenräume* (Stuttgart, 1928).

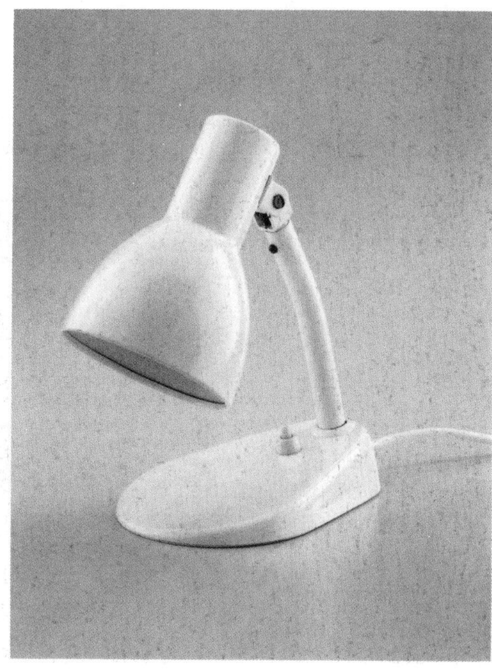

46 MARIANNE BRANDT AND HIN BRENDENDIECK
"Kandem" bedside lamp, 1928. Made by Körting & Matthieson, Leipzig. Lacquered steel. Height approx. 9⅞" (25 cm). Bauhaus-Archiv, Berlin.

47 Hanging lamps, c. 1926–27, (from left) by Marianne Brandt and Brandt and Hans Przyrembel, both made at the Bauhaus metal workshop, Dessau; and by W. H. Gispen, Rotterdam. Metal and glass. From Werner Gräff, ed., *Innenräume* (Stuttgart, 1928).

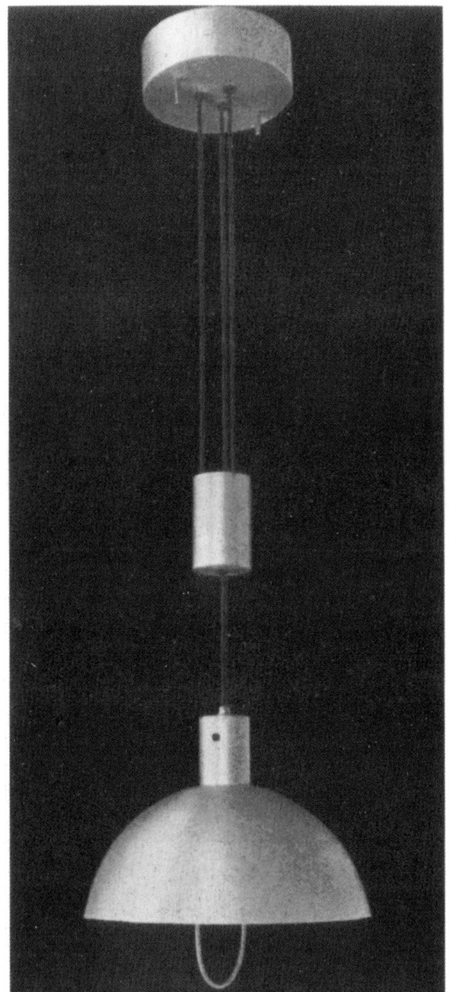

> Let us be frank:
> I draw a shelf with glasses on it; a shelf
> with plates, soup plates, etc.; a shelf with bottles, pitchers, etc. Drawers with automatic storage of silverware. . . .
> I draw a shelf with linens, sheets, towels, etc., a shelf with underwear, drawers with lingerie, stockings, etc.
> I draw a shelf with shoes, a shelf with hats.
> I draw clothing hung on a clothes hook; a dress.
> That's all.
> The inventory of objects we use is complete.
> These objects are in proportion to our limbs, are adapted to our gestures.
> They have a *common scale*, they fit into a module [fig. 48].[19]

Simple and efficient and quintessentially functionalist, modular storage systems such as this could be fabricated in any material and at any price level. A similar approach had been taken as early as 1917 by the Danish architect and designer Kaare Klint, who derived the proportions of office furnishings by using standard sizes of letter paper and forms and later went on to analyze in great detail the variations of human proportion and the dimensions and

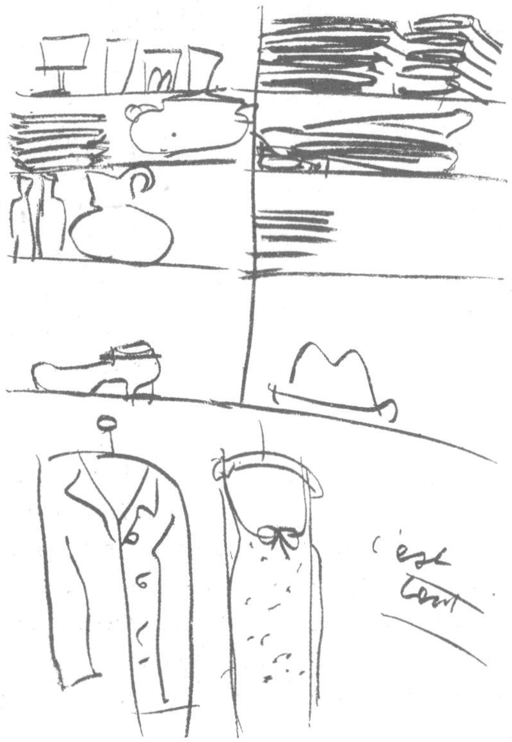

48 LE CORBUSIER
"That's all." From
Précisions (Paris, 1930).

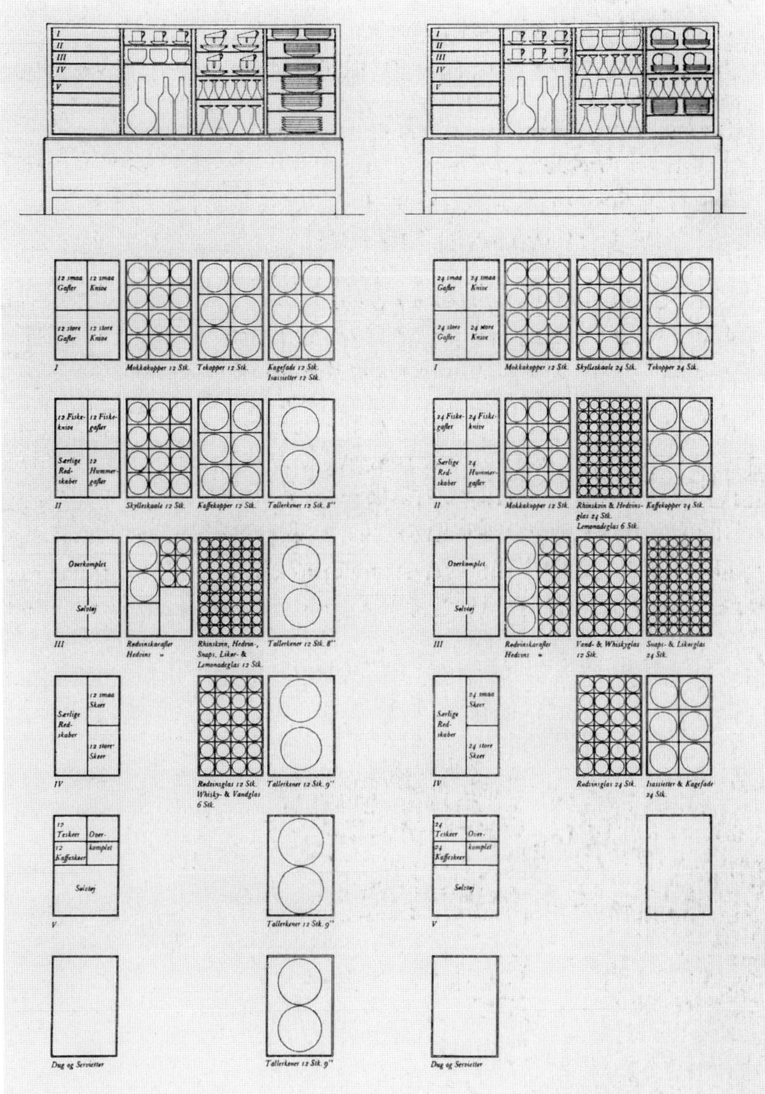

49 KAARE KLINT
Analysis of various possibilities for the storage of standard tableware services within a sideboard, 1929.

quantities of objects in daily use in Denmark to create the bases for standardized storage units and furniture systems (fig. 49).[20] Le Corbusier used his cabinets liberally to enhance his own architectural conceptions. In the Paris pavilion, they were made of painted wood in two versions, as tall built-ins and as shorter units mounted on tubular-metal legs (fig. 40), where they defined separate areas within its open plan. At Weissenhof his built-in modular closets were even more architecturally integrated to create a sequence of private sleeping areas (fig. 44).

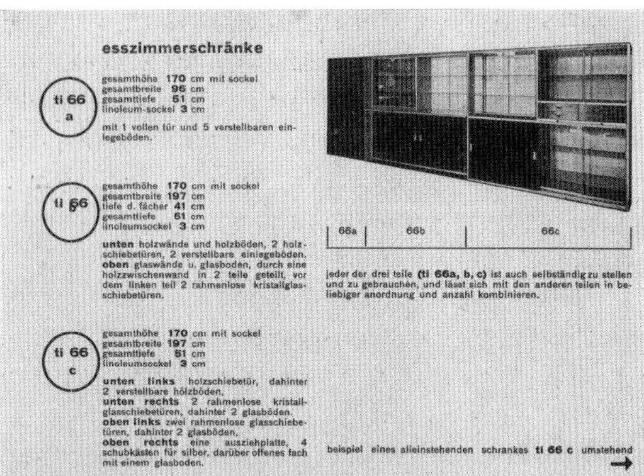

esszimmerschränke

ti 66 a

gesamthöhe **170** cm mit sockel
gesamtbreite **96** cm
gesamttiefe **51** cm
linoleum-sockel **3** cm

mit 1 vollen tür und 5 verstellbaren einlegeböden.

ti 66 b

gesamthöhe **170** cm mit sockel
gesamtbreite **197** cm
tiefe d. fächer **41** cm
gesamttiefe **51** cm
linoleumsockel **3** cm

unten holzwände und holzböden, 2 holzschiebetüren, 2 verstellbare einlegeböden. **oben** glaswände u. glasboden, durch eine holzzwischenwand in 2 teile geteilt, vor dem linken teil 2 rahmenlose kristallglasschiebetüren.

ti 66 c

gesamthöhe **170** cm mit sockel
gesamtbreite **197** cm
gesamttiefe **51** cm
linoleumsockel **3** cm

unten links holzschiebetür, dahinter 2 verstellbare holzböden,
unten rechts 2 rahmenlose kristallglasschiebetüren, dahinter 2 glasböden.
oben links zwei rahmenlose glasschiebetüren, dahinter 2 glasböden,
oben rechts eine ausziehplatte, 4 schubkästen für silber, darüber offenes fach mit einem glasboden.

jeder der drei teile **(ti 66a, b, c)** ist auch selbständig zu stellen und zu gebrauchen, und lässt sich mit den anderen teilen in beliebiger anordnung und anzahl kombinieren.

beispiel eines alleinstehenden schrankes **ti 66 c** umstehend →

50 Brochure for Marcel Breuer's modular furniture, from 1925, Bauhaus, Dessau (1926–27).

Marcel Breuer, director of the furniture workshop at the Bauhaus, also took up the concept of modular cabinetwork about 1925 with a system of wooden components that he used at Weissenhof. Manufactured by the Bauhaus and promoted in a brochure published in 1926–27 (fig. 50), they were based on a thirty-three centimeter module (fig. 51) and could be ordered in a variety of natural and painted finishes, with compartments left open or fitted with wooden or glass doors. At Weissenhof they were configured as stacked components set on the floor,[21] but more frequently they were combined in single and double units as wall-hung cabinets, and they could be mounted on tubular-steel legs as well.

Another, more encompassing modular system went beyond storage to include a full suite of living- and dining-room furniture (fig. 53). Created by Erich Dieckmann, a Bauhaus student who after the school's move to Dessau in 1926 had remained in Weimar with its successor, the Staatliche Hochschule für Handwerk und Baukunst, the system had been designed and made there as an example of inexpensive, standard furnishing for small apartments to be submitted to the German industrial standards institute. This *Typenmöbel* system, made of oak or cherry, related the sizes of chairs, tables, and cupboards to particular functions based on an ideal human measurement using a nine-centimeter module, as Dieckmann demonstrated in schematic drawings in a 1931 monograph of his work (fig. 52).[22]

The most rudimentary of the standardized production furniture at Weissenhof was that designed by Max Hoene, a sculptor from Munich, on commission from the Bayerische Hausrathilfe. Hoene had already created a basic range of items for this welfare agency, attempting to bring variety to even the lowest level of factory-produced household furnishings through the different groupings that could be achieved with add-on components, which were colored with lacquer and stains to individualize and enhance their blocklike forms (fig. 54).[23] At the other end of the spectrum was the line of varnished oak furniture developed for Weissenhof by Adolf G. Schneck, professor at the Kunstgewerbeschule in Stuttgart (who had been director of the 1924 Werkbund exhibition "Die Form"). Called "Die Billige Wohnung" (The Low-Cost Home), a name that plainly announced its purpose (fig. 55), it had been commissioned by the Deutsche Werkstätten in Hellerau (Dresden), and was said by Ernst Zimmermann to be "everything the younger generation desires," displaying the "clearest expression of the modern feeling of our time."[24] The series, conceived for large-scale production and wide appeal, in-

51 MARCEL BREUER
Diagram of modular furniture system, from 1925. Bauhaus-Archiv, Berlin.

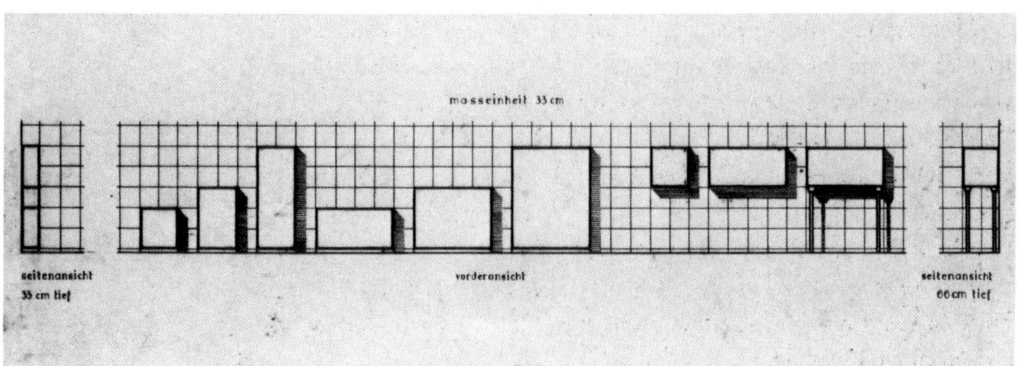

cluded suites for the living room, dining room (fig. 56), bedroom, and study. Some sixty to seventy of the Werkstätten's woodworkers were able to turn out one hundred bedroom suites a week. While relatively inexpensive, the furniture was made of solid wood, not veneers or plywood, and executed with a high quality of workmanship (colorplate 4), which Schneck believed was the only way that standardized furnishings could achieve mass sales.[25]

The furniture of Ferdinand Kramer (fig. 57) was highly praised for its novelty. His light and mobile pieces were from three rooms of standardized plywood furnishings that had brought him first prize in a competition in 1925 for the Frankfurt Hausrat, an organization that distributed household goods to the unemployed.[26] The journal of the Deutscher Werkbund, *Die Form*, called his furniture "classics in a contemporary vein" instilled "with the modern sense of style." "With intense concentration," the critic Paul Renner wrote, "he thinks through the issues of practicality and of potential innovations in material and technique. His furniture represents the last word in comfort.... [It] is the best domestic equipment imaginable for the simple, cubic ... rooms of the modern house."[27]

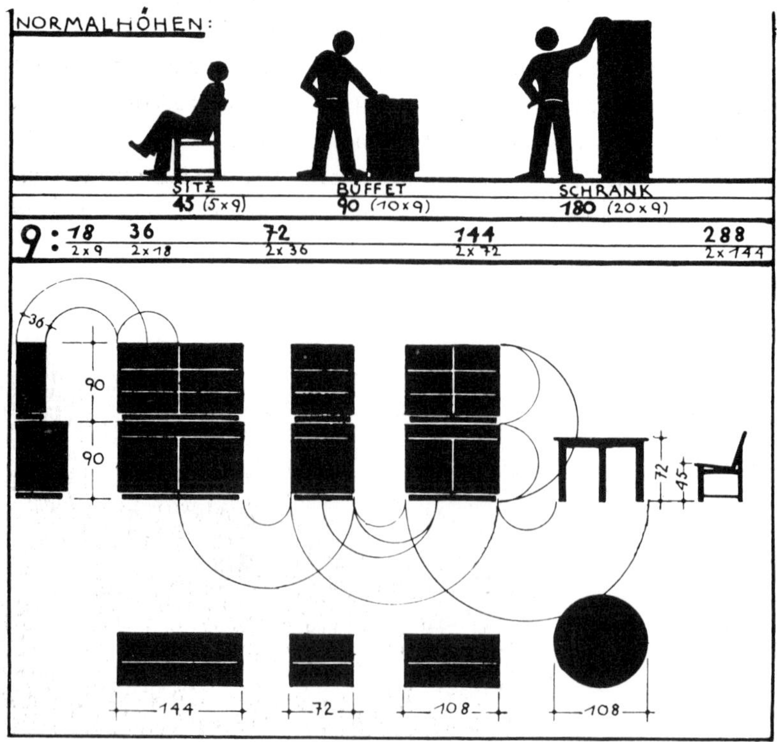

52 ERICH DIECKMANN
Diagram of module for standard furniture for living and dining room. From Erich Dieckmann, *Möbelbau in Holz, Rohr und Stahl* (Stuttgart, 1931).

53 ERICH DIECKMANN
Study corner in apartment house by Ludwig Mies van der Rohe at Weissenhofsiedlung, Stuttgart, 1927. Bauhaus-Archiv, Berlin.

The assessment of Kramer's practical and stylish although not revolutionary furniture as the "best domestic equipment imaginable" for contemporary interiors may seem overblown today, but on the basis of utility and comfort, rather than style and the now-entrenched association of modern design with metal and the machine, his thoughtful, practical work perhaps deserves this distinction. While the wooden furniture shown at Weissenhof may have been stylistically conservative, as some have characterized it, much of it de-

54 MAX HOENE
Children's dining set. From Werner Gräff, ed., *Innenräume* (Stuttgart, 1928).

DIE BILLIGE WOHNUNG

NACH ENTWÜRFEN VON
PROF. ADOLF G. SCHNECK
STUTTGART

DEUTSCHE
WERKSTÄTTEN A/G

HELLERAU · DRESDEN · BERLIN · MÜNCHEN

55 Catalogue for Adolf G. Schneck's *Die Billige Wohnung* series, 1927, Deutsche Werkstätten (Hellerau, 1928).

56 ADOLF G. SCHNECK
Sideboard from *Die Billige Wohnung* series, 1927. Made by the Deutsche Werkstätten, Hellerau (Dresden). Kunstgewerbemuseum Berlin.

57 FERDINAND KRAMER
Living-dining room in apartment house by Ludwig Mies van der Rohe at Weissenhofsiedlung, Stuttgart, 1927.

pendent on solid Arts and Crafts values,[28] there can be no doubt that the modular systems and relatively low-cost production were forward-looking, as demonstrated by the great increase in production and popularity of such systems in the decades that followed.

The tubular-steel furniture of Marcel Breuer, which was also shown at Weissenhof, was a totally independent and deliberate approach to problems of rationalization, industrial production, and distribution, cast in a medium that had a new and distinctly modern presence. For Breuer, as he wrote in *Innenräume*, the functionalist "yardstick" of rationality, economy, and mass availability implicit in his club chair of 1925 (colorplate 7) was as important as its formal design and the properties of the material he was exploring:

> Two years ago, when I saw the finished version of my first steel club armchair, I thought that this out of all my work would bring me the most criticism. It is my most extreme work both in its outward appearance and in the use of materials; it is the least artistic, the most logical, the least "cosy" and the most mechanical.
>
> What happened was precisely the opposite of what I had expected. The interest shown in both modernist and non-modernist circles showed me clearly that contemporary attitudes were undergoing a change, abandoning the whimsical in favour of the rational. . . .

58 WALTER GROPIUS
Living room in house at Weissenhofsiedlung, Stuttgart, 1927, with furniture by Marcel Breuer. Bauhaus-Archiv, Berlin.

> A chair made of high-grade steel tubing (a highly elastic material) with tightly stretched fabric in the appropriate places, makes a light, completely self-sprung seat which is as comfortable as an upholstered chair, but is many times lighter, handier and more hygienic, and therefore many times more practical in use....
>
> The severe rationalisation of components—the use of the same components in different types of furniture, the possibility of reducing them to two-dimensional parts (over fifty club armchairs can be packed into a space of one cubic metre, with obvious advantages for transport), and a full regard for industrial and manufacturing considerations all contributed to the social yardstick of a price which could be paid by the broadest possible mass of the population. And I might say that without meeting this yardstick, I could not have found the project particularly satisfactory.[29]

Regardless of his emphasis on production, the club chair was primarily a formal tour-de-force; constructed from welded tubular steel, the material he had admired in his new bicycle, and refined over a period of several months from early awkward versions with four separate legs into the classic model with runners, which made it both light and easily movable, his chair gave the impression of having been made of a single piece of extruded steel. The planes of fabric stretched over the steel tubing and bound within its open cubic shape still reflected very much an involvement with the relationship of pri-

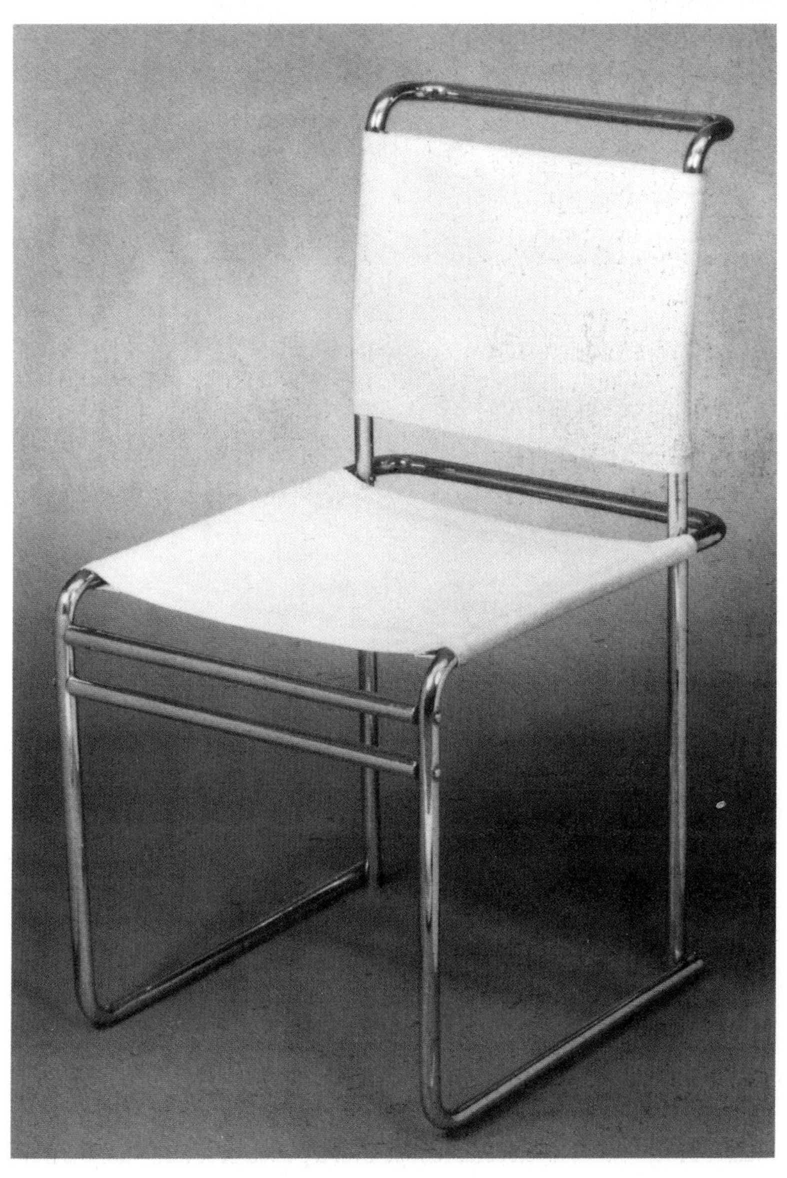

59 MARCEL BREUER
Chair, 1926–27. Made by Gebrüder Thonet.
Steel and fabric. Height 33¾″ (85.5 cm). The Brooklyn Museum, New York.
Gift of Mr. and Mrs. Alexis Zalstem-Zalessky.

mary forms influenced by Cubism and the De Stijl designers, particularly the work of Rietveld, which had held sway over Breuer and the Bauhaus in the early 1920s. Breuer's subsequent tubular-steel chairs (fig. 59), stools, and tables (colorplate 6), which were used in large numbers to furnish Gropius's new Bauhaus building in Dessau and the house he designed for Weissenhof (fig. 58), were more restricted in their vision, the extreme planar inventiveness abandoned for the goals of manufacturing efficiency and practicality. They are more closely tied to his concept of "metal furniture [as] part of a modern room," which he outlined in an article in 1928: "It is 'styleless,' for it is expected not to express any particular styling beyond its purpose and the construction necessary therefore."[30]

Notes

1 Le Corbusier, *L'Art décoratif d'aujourd'hui* [1925], rev. ed. (Paris: Éditions Vincent, Fréal & Cie., 1959), p. 67.

2 See Karin Kirsch, *The Weissenhofsiedlung: Experimental Housing Built for the Deutscher Werkbund, Stuttgart, 1927* (New York: Rizzoli, 1989); and Richard Pommer and Christian F. Otto, *Weissenhof 1927 and the Modern Movement in Architecture* (Chicago and London: The University of Chicago Press, 1991).

3 Ludwig Mies van der Rohe, in *Bau und Wohnung* (Stuttgart: Akad. Verlag Dr. Fr. Wedekind & Co., 1927), p. 77; translated in Kirsch, *Weissenhofsiedlung*, p. 47.

4 See Siegfried Giedion, *Mechanization Takes Command: A Contribution to Anonymous History* (New York: Oxford University Press, 1948).

5 Peter Behrens, *Berliner Tageblatt*, August 29, 1907; translated as "Art in Technology," in Tilmann Buddensieg, *Industriekultur: Peter Behrens and the AEG, 1907–1914* (Cambridge, Mass., and London: The MIT Press, 1984), p. 208.

6 Ernst Zimmermann, "Künstlerische Maschinenmöbel," *Deutsche Kunst und Dekoration* 17 (1906), p. 263; quoted in Kathryn B. Hiesinger, ed., *Art Nouveau in Munich: Masters of Jugendstil* (Philadelphia: Philadelphia Museum of Art in association with Prestel, 1988), p. 140.

7 L. Deubner, "German Architecture and Decoration," in *"The Studio" Yearbook of Decorative Art* (London, 1914), pp. 93–94.

8 Hermann Muthesius, "Propositions"; translated in Charlotte Benton, ed., *Documents: A Collection of Source Material on the Modern Movement* (Milton Keynes, England: The Open University Press, 1975), p. 5.

9 Walter Gropius, *Idee und Aufbau des Staatlichen Bauhauses Weimar* (Munich: Bauhausverlag, 1923); translated as "The Theory and Organization of the Bauhaus," in Herbert Bayer, Walter Gropius, and Ise Gropius, eds., *Bauhaus, 1919–1928* (New York: The Museum of Modern Art, 1938), p. 22.

10 Walter Gropius, "Bauhaus Dessau—Principles of Bauhaus Production" [1926], in Hans M. Wingler, *The Bauhaus: Weimar Dessau Berlin Chicago* (Cambridge, Mass., and London: The MIT Press, 1969), p. 110.

11 Le Corbusier, *Towards a New Architecture*, translated by Frederick Etchells (London: John Rodker Publisher, 1927), pp. 141–42.

12 Le Corbusier, *The Decorative Art of Today*, translated by James I. Dunnett (Cambridge, Mass.: The MIT Press, 1987), p. 91.

13 Le Corbusier actually had to have the standard Maple & Company chairs remade at a smaller scale to fit through the narrow doors of the pavilion.

14 See Le Corbusier, *Decorative Art*, p. 76n.

15 Gropius, "Bauhaus Dessau," in Wingler, *The Bauhaus*, p. 109.

16 Werner Gräff, ed., *Innenräume* (Stuttgart: Akad. Verlag Dr. Fr. Wedekind & Co., 1928).

17 See Pommer and Otto, *Weissenhof 1927*, p. 125.

18 Le Corbusier, ed., *Almanach d'architecture moderne* (Paris: Les Éditions G. Crès et Cie., 1926), p. 145; see also pp. 109–13, "Un Seul Corps de métier."

19 Le Corbusier, "The Undertaking of Furniture" [1929], in *Precisions on the Present State of Architecture and City Planning* (Cambridge, Mass., and London: The MIT Press, 1991), p. 111.

20 See Rigmor Andersen, *Kaare Klint: Møbler* (Copenhagen: Kunstakademiet, 1979).

21 In his interior for the house designed by Mart Stam; see Kirsch, *Weissenhofsiedlung*, reproduced p. 175.

22 Erich Dieckmann, *Möbelbau in Holz, Rohr und Stahl* (Stuttgart: Julius Hoffmann Verlag, 1931).

23 See Kirsch, *Weissenhofsiedlung*, pp. 65–66.

24 Ernst Zimmermann, "Die ersten deutschen Möbel in Fliessarbeit," *Deutsche Kunst und Dekoration* 60 (September 1927), p. 422.

25 Adolf G. Schneck, "Über Typenmöbel," in Gräff, *Innenräume*, pp. 131–32; translated in Kirsch, *Weissenhofsiedlung*, p. 67.

26 See Claude Lichtenstein, *Ferdinand Kramer: Der Charme des Systematischen* (Giessen, Germany: Anabas Verlag, 1991), pp. 158–60, 173.

27 Paul Renner, *Die Form* 2 (October 1927), p. 322; translated in Kirsch, *Weissenhofsiedlung*, p. 59.

28 See Pommer and Otto, *Weissenhof 1927*, p. 130.

29 Marcel Breuer, "Metallmöbel," in Gräff, *Innenräume*, pp. 133–34; translated as "Metal Furniture," in Tim Benton and Charlotte Benton, with Dennis Sharp, eds., *Form and Function: A Source Book for the History of Architecture and Design 1890–1939* (London: Crosby Lockwood Staples in association with the Open University Press, 1975), pp. 226–27.

30 Marcel Breuer, "Metallmöbel und moderne Räumlichkeit," *Das Neue Frankfurt*, January 1928, p. 11; translated as "Metal Furniture and Modern Accommodation," in Württembergischer Kunstverein, Stuttgart, *50 Years Bauhaus* (1968), p. 109.

Revolution in Metal

This metal furniture is intended to be nothing but a necessary apparatus for contemporary life.

Marcel Breuer[1]

In an exchange of articles in 1929, *The Studio* confronted its readers with the question "Wood or Metal?" (fig. 60), with the English critic John Gloag speaking out on the side of wood ("Metal," he wrote, "is cold and brutally hard, and . . . it gives no comfort to the eye.") and Charlotte Perriand, the young associate who had joined Le Corbusier's architectural firm the previous year, rebutting ("Metal plays the same part in furniture as cement has done in architecture. IT IS A REVOLUTION.").[2] The question need not have been asked, for metal had already won hands down, if only for its stylish novelty. It had become the universal constant of modern design, not limited to any single viewpoint or orthodoxy. Suddenly wood seemed conservative, any of its prior associations with modernism ignored. Even such designs as the pioneering, versatile, laminated-wood furniture created for mass production at the Bauhaus under Gropius's successor, the Swiss architect Hannes Meyer—whose social philosophy emphasized standard types based on real

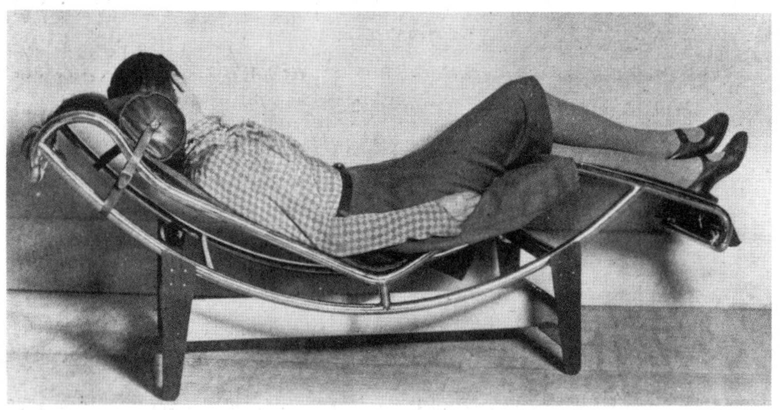

Metal Couch designed by Le Corbusier, Pierre Jeanneret and Charlotte Perriand

WOOD OR METAL?

60 Charlotte Perriand, "Wood or Metal?" From *The Studio* (1929).

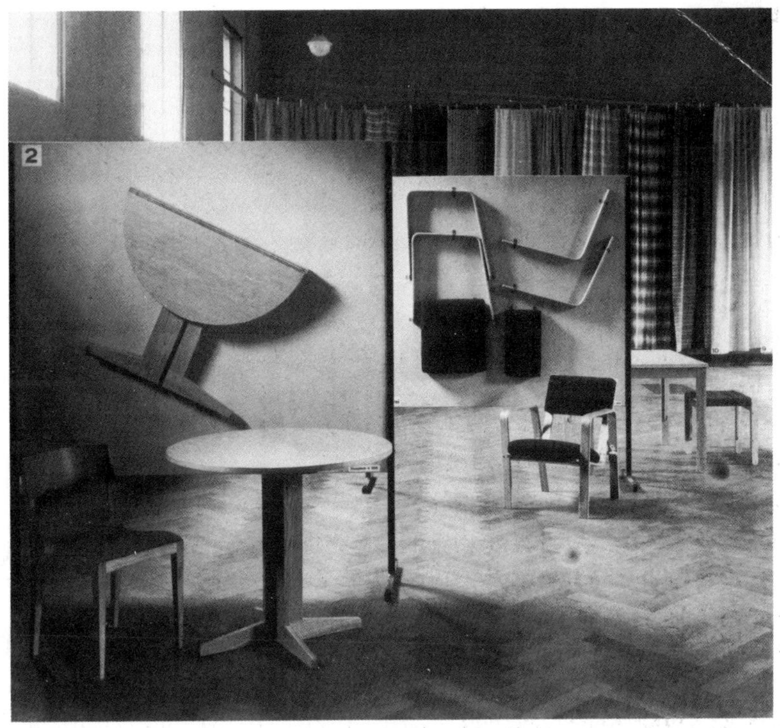

61 Bauhaus touring exhibition at the Kunsthalle, Basel, 1929, showing Josef Albers's armchair, c. 1929, and Gustav Hassenpflug's folding table, 1928.

needs and on function, not form—such as Josef Albers's knock-down armchair and Gustav Hassenpflug's collapsible table (fig. 61), were denied their due. Not until after Alvar Aalto's innovative work with molded laminated wood in Finland became known during the 1930s was wood invested once again with significant connotations of modernism.

When with the help of a plumber Marcel Breuer had first produced his tubular-steel club chair in 1925 (colorplate 7), he introduced a new material into the vocabulary of modern furniture, and his work has been much and justly celebrated as a turning point in twentieth-century design. Its impact was immediate, and just two years later, a large representation of metal furniture appeared at the Weissenhof exhibition in Stuttgart, although by no means did all of it follow his concern for standardization and ease of production and distribution. Included was the first modern-style chair designed on the principle of the cantilever (fig. 62), an invention of the Dutch architect Mart Stam that further challenged the properties of this material. Stam had taken the form of Breuer's tubular-metal frame with runners but interrupted it, eliminating the back leg and supporting the seat from the front only, to create a daring new furniture type. The history of the cantilever chair had

62 MART STAM
Table and chair, c. 1927.
From Werner Gräff, ed., *Innenräume* (Stuttgart, 1928).

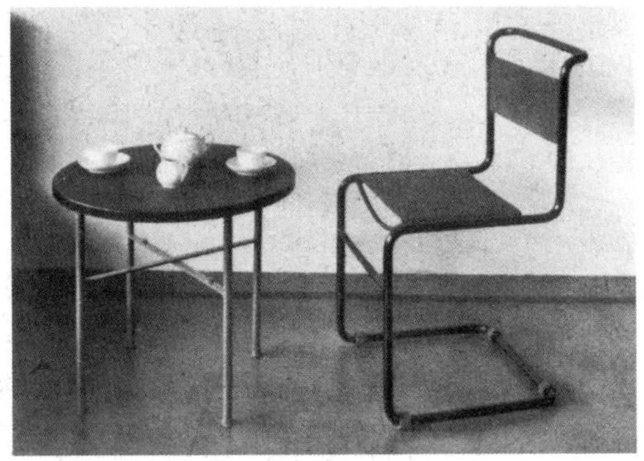

been mired in confusion for a long time, but with the comprehensive documentation recently published, the design precedence and importance of Mart Stam was finally clarified.[3] Stam's idea was quickly adapted by others, among them Ludwig Mies van der Rohe, who accepted the precedents of both Breuer's original use of tubular metal and Stam's cantilever and filed for a separate patent for his own considerably more elegant and resilient version, on the basis that he had been "the first to have exploited consistently the spring quality of steel tubes."[4] Mies's chair (colorplate 5), also part of the furnishings in Stuttgart, was distinguished by large curved semicircular legs that give slightly under the weight of the sitter (the curve repeated in the version with arms).

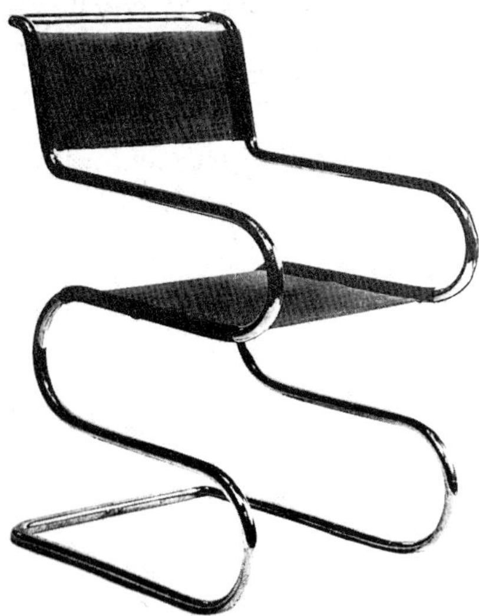

63 Armchair, 1930.
Made by Thonet Frères.
Steel and cloth.

64 RENÉ HERBST Armchair, 1928.
Steel and upholstery. Height 26″ (66 cm).

Today there is a tendency to think of the few classic examples of metal furniture that are being manufactured again as representative of the output of the period, but nothing could be further from the truth. It seems that from the beginning anyone who could, did experiment with metal, and designs of all kinds were created and sold, some so far removed from the geometry of Breuer and so extreme in their fantasy of what could be achieved in this strong, resilient material that Stam dubbed them "steel macaroni monsters" (fig. 63).[5] The notice on the Salon des Artistes Décorateurs in Paris published in *The Studio* in 1928 confirmed this explosion in production: "The outstanding feature this year is the definite entry of metal into the domain of furnishing. There are some fifty exhibitors (not the least important) who use steel tubes for chairs."[6] The French took a different approach from the Germans; it was not enough for them to applaud metal as the material that responded "the best to the modern imperatives of comfort, hygiene, cleanliness, and simplicity"; it was for them, according to the reviewer for *Art et Décoration*, both a "constructive and decorative element"[7] out of which new forms had been born (fig. 64).

65 Advertisement for YSY Metal Tube Furniture, 1932. From *Kokusai Kenchiku* (March 1932). National Diet Library, Tokyo.

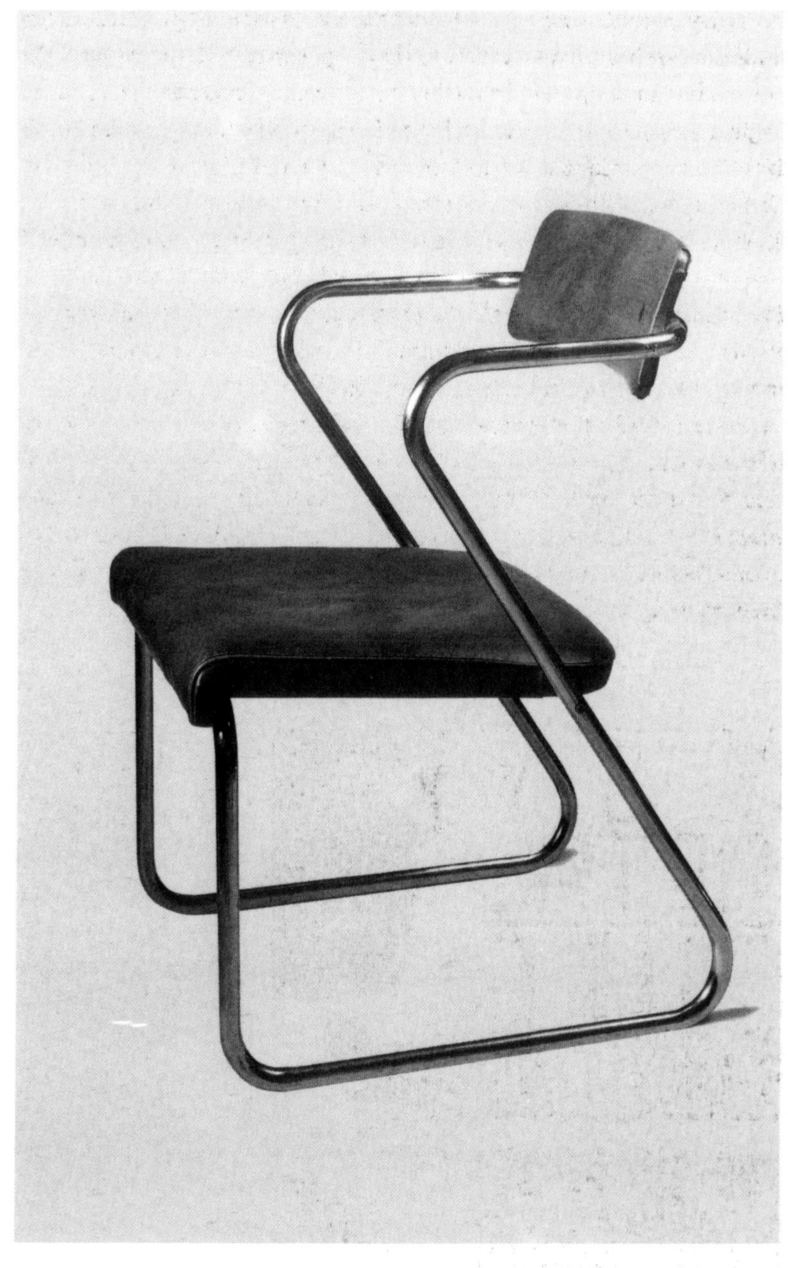

66 GILBERT ROHDE Armchair, c. 1931.
Made by Troy Sunshade Company, Troy, Ohio.
Steel and plywood with upholstery. Height 31½″ (77 cm).
Baltimore Museum of Art. Friends of Art Fund.

As early as 1928 the manufacture of Western-style tubular-steel furniture had begun in Japan;[8] frames, fabrication methods, and upholstery materials were carefully studied and then directly copied, and by 1932 a large collection of imitation-European metal furniture was being produced (fig. 65). In the United States the onslaught of metal was delayed. In 1930 *Home & Field* reported that aside from custom production, metal furniture could be had from only three retail sources in New York.[9] This would quickly change as American manufacturers latched onto the up-and-coming style, arranging to import European, mostly French, models and to have native designs put into production. American tubular-metal furniture was generally either of a pedestrian, commercial variety or, influenced by the French examples, it adhered to the Moderne and Streamline styles, such as those of Donald Deskey and Gilbert Rohde (fig. 66).

Not only did the number and variety of metal designs proliferate internationally but sales also grew enormously, with the leading European manufacturer of metal furniture, Thonet, proudly publishing a graph in its 1934 catalogue to demonstrate the rapid increase in its production (fig. 67). It is not surprising that Thonet, founded by the nineteenth-century inventor of the bentwood process, would recognize the economic advantages of bent steel.[10] In 1928 Thonet purchased its first tubular-steel designs, and the following year began to consolidate the manufacture of this furniture under its

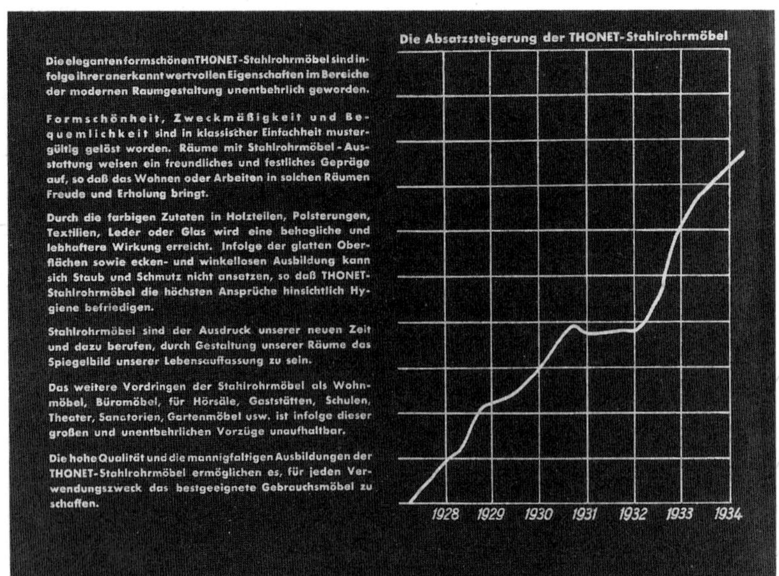

67 "The increase in sales of Thonet tubular-steel furniture." From *Thonet Stahlrohrmöbel* catalogue, 1934. Vitra Design Museum, Weil am Rhein, Germany.

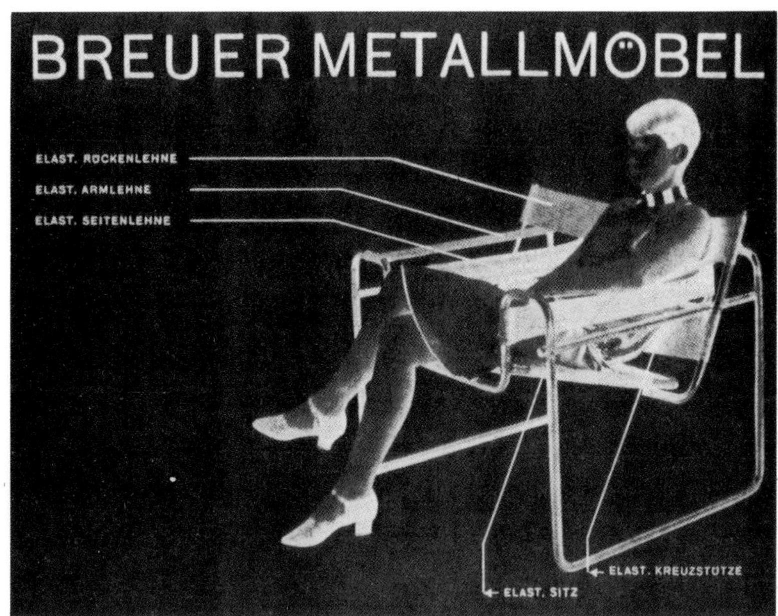

68 *Breuer Metallmöbel*, 1927. Cover of Standard-Möbel catalogue designed by Herbert Bayer. Bauhaus, Dessau.

roof by acquiring the Standard-Möbel company. Standard-Möbel was a partnership that Marcel Breuer had entered to take over the production and marketing of his metal furniture, which initially had been carried out independently in his own workshop. Standard-Möbel's first catalogue, entitled *Breuer Metallmöbel* (1927), illustrated eight of Breuer's seating and table designs and included a didactic representation of his club chair on the cover (fig. 68). Thonet's first catalogue of metal furniture in 1929 was likewise devoted exclusively to Breuer's work, and his designs, including chairs (frontispiece), tables, shelves, a bed, and a tea cart, were also prominent in Thonet's larger 1930–31 catalogue of tubular-steel furniture, "designed by well-known architects and . . . characterized by correct and functional forms."[11] It also included the two versions of Mies van der Rohe's cantilever chair shown at Weissenhof; a group of designs from France acquired by Thonet's branch in Paris, among them the joint work of Le Corbusier, Pierre Jeanneret, and Charlotte Perriand, and that of the architects Béwé (Bruno Weill) and A. Guyot and the architect-designer André Lurçat, as well as a number of unattributed pieces for office and home. The mix was suggested by the desks, tables, and chairs illustrated on the cover (fig. 69), but what was meant by the phrase "correct and functional forms" was left to the client to decide, for Thonet's metal production was far from committed to any strict philosophy of design.

69 Cover of *Thonet Stahlrohrmöbel* catalogue, 1930–31. Bauhaus, Dessau.

The Le Corbusier-Jeanneret-Perriand metal furniture shown in the catalogue had been exhibited first in 1928 and again in 1929, when it was included in the "Interior Equipment of a Dwelling" presentation sponsored by Thonet at the Salon d'Automne in Paris (fig. 70). Overseeing the furniture and interior designs for the firm had been left to Perriand, who in a later interview described the circumstances of their design and production and how the firm had become involved with Thonet:

> Le Corbusier had no time for what he called "le blah blah blah"; he detested it. So when I arrived, he set me to work straight away on his theme of *casiers* (storage systems), metal chairs and tables—the ideas he had published in his books.... From 1927 to 1937, I was responsible for everything concerning "l'équipement" (furniture and fitting out).... Le Corbusier always interested himself in the "why" of things–the different ways of sitting, what sort of chairs we need, what pose they should cater for. His contributions to the 1929 *chaise longue* [colorplate 9] were sketches [fig. 71] showing the position of a person lying with feet in the air—the relaxed pose one takes with one's feet up, as if against the trunk of a tree.... We made all the prototypes ourselves—that was my job.... We had no money for our exhibition at the 1929 Salon d'Automne, so we tried to find an "*éditeur*" for the fur-

> niture designs. Thonet undertook that role and thereby covered the exhibition costs. He took our prototypes after the exhibition and manufactured from them on a small scale, but as they were never put into mass production, our chairs were always relatively expensive.[12]

Shown as stylized, rudimentary depictions in Le Corbusier's drawings over the previous years, such as a pastel for the house commissioned by the Church family (colorplate 8), and refined under Perriand's direction, these designs were an attempt to create modern versions of the standard furniture types that he had promoted earlier. They included a light armchair, club chair, chaise longue, and a table. The club chair, an updated version of the comfortable nineteenth-century Morris chair called by the designers the "Grand Confort" and a replacement for the Maple & Company chair Le Corbusier had frequently used, was composed of five cushions held within a cubic, cagelike tubular-steel frame; the structure, usually hidden within the cushioning of such chairs, was revealed as part of the design itself (colorplate 19). The adjustable armchair (fig. 72), with a light, open frame and a pivoting back rest (shown in the pastel sketch in a version with a runner across the front), was based on a popular type of nineteenth-century "nomadic" or disassemblable chair with a wooden frame and canvas or leather seats used by the

70 LE CORBUSIER, PIERRE JEANNERET, AND CHARLOTTE PERRIAND
"Interior Equipment of a Dwelling" installation, Salon d'Automne, Paris, 1929. From *Art et Décoration* (December, 1929). Victoria & Albert Museum, London.

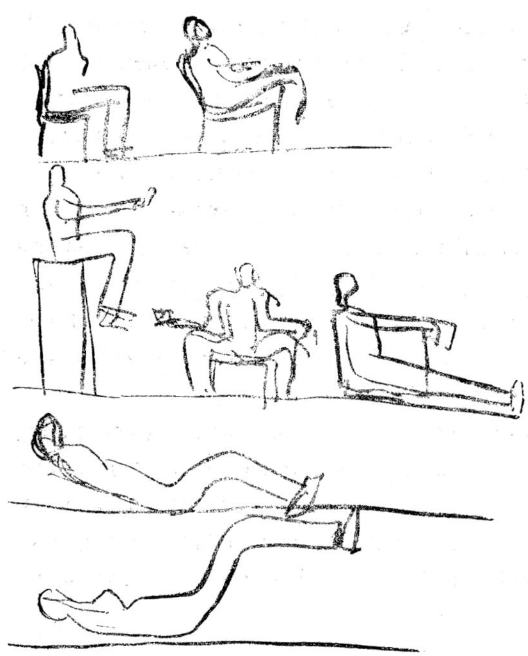

71 LE CORBUSIER
"Positions for sitting." From *Précisions* (Paris, 1930).

military and travelers and known in many variants. The chaise longue (colorplate 9) was less specific in its antecedents, but looked back to Victorian sofas made to conform to the shape of the reclining body, adjustable medical chairs, and other seating that favored the voguish idea that sitting with the feet elevated was one of the most healthful and relaxing positions. The merits of the chaise longue, constructed of a frame of tubular steel set onto a sheet-metal base, were described by Le Corbusier: "Here is the machine for resting. We built it with bicycle tubes and covered it with a magnificent pony skin; it is light enough to be pushed by foot, can be manipulated by a child; I thought of the western cowboy smoking his pipe, his feet up above his head, leaning against a fireplace: complete restfulness. Our chaise longue takes all positions, my weight alone is enough to keep it in the chosen position; no mechanism. It is the true machine for resting."[13]

The relative paucity of original examples of early tubular-steel furniture and our dependence on black-and-white photographs for historic views have skewed our understanding both of their original settings and of how they actually looked—that is, how they were finished and upholstered. Their postwar resurgence, clothed in a new aesthetic and designed for new surroundings that are familiar to us, has confused this even further. Following his penchant for defining interiors with colors according to an elaborate program based on the precepts of Purism, Le Corbusier's pastel drawing for the Villa Church (colorplate 8) shows how deliberately he used color to define the volumes of his interiors. Other such specific indications from the period are found in descriptions in exhibition reviews, in a few color illustrations in magazines, and in advertising materials and catalogues. A review in *Art et Décoration* imagined that Charlotte Perriand's dining room at the 1928 Salon (colorplate 10) "would charm a Brillat-Savarin . . . with its gaiety, its comforts so well adapted to the pleasure of the table and of good company. Her revolving metal chairs, furnished with cushions of coral red leather, her stools topped with green, and her retractable table, notably create ingenious and charming solutions to the problems of decorating."[14]

A Thonet brochure for Breuer's furniture "system" from 1931, promoting its chairs with seats of red, orange, blue, and green (colorplate 11), conveys some sense of their colors at the time. The 1930–31 Thonet catalogue confirms this boldness and variety of color: it lists gray, rust, brown, orange, red, green, blue, black, and yellow as the dyes available for the stretched fabric

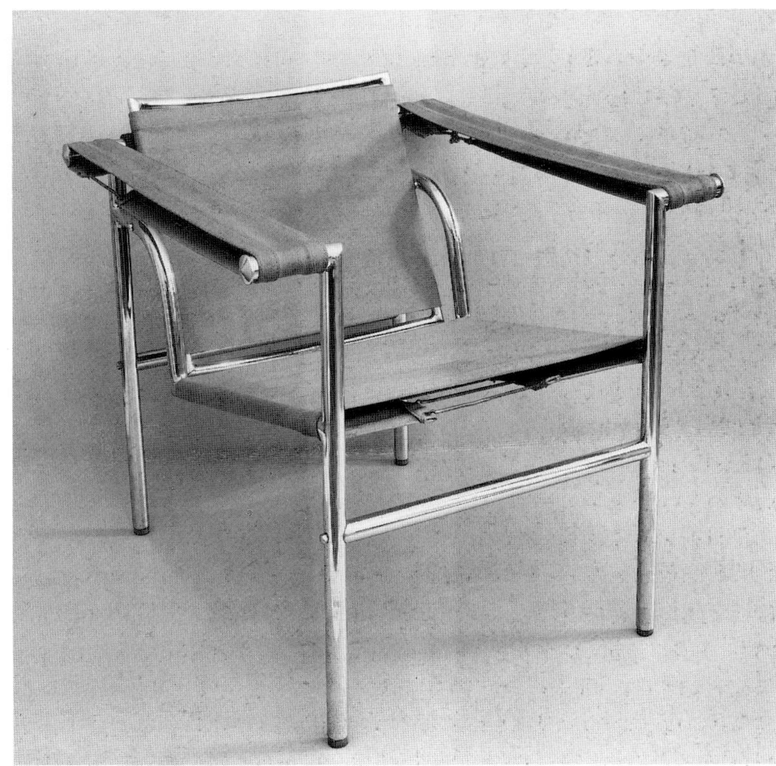

72 LE CORBUSIER, PIERRE JEANNERET, AND CHARLOTTE PERRIAND
Armchair with adjustable back, 1928. Made by Thonet Frères. Chrome-plated steel and canvas. Height 26 1/8" (66.3 cm). The Museum of Modern Art, New York. Gift of Thonet Frères.

upholstery, which was an especially durable weave called *Eisengarn* (iron cloth). Color was likewise a standard option for wooden parts (which could be colored to match the fabrics) and for the tubular frames (colorplate 12). Thonet offered two quite different metal finishes, chrome-plated and lacquered, whose virtues were both carefully described in the catalogue:

> CHROME-PLATED. The precision steel tubes out of which our tubular steel furniture is made are first copper-plated, then nickel and eventually chrome. Considering today's technical standards chrome-plating guarantees optimum protection against rust and should thus be preferred to a simple nickel-plating. Chrome-plated tubular steel furniture has a platinum-like, subtle blueish-white colour and a shiny surface....
>
> LACQUERED. In this version the tubular steel is treated in a specific chemical process. The lacquer offers excellent rust prevention. Furthermore, it renders the furniture resistant to bumping and scratching. This type of tubular steel furniture can be delivered in the following colours: lacquer red, brick red, lemon, cream, green, blue, violet, chocolate, silver grey, white, black, and pea green as well as in a silver and gold bronze.[15]

The use of such colors for metal cannot be dismissed as a marketing tool of the manufacturer, for the designers themselves chose colored frames for furniture that decorated their own interiors. One reason Charlotte Perriand gave for opting for metal over wood was that "the protective coatings against toxic agencies not only lower the cost of upkeep, but have a considerable AESTHETIC value.... AESTHETICS OF METAL. Aluminium varnish, Duco, Parkerisation [rust proofing], Paint, all provide variety in the treatment of metal. If we use metal in conjunction with leather for chairs, with marble slabs, glass and india-rubber for tables, floor coverings, cement, vegetable substances, we get a range of wonderful combinations and new aesthetic effects."[16] A manuscript repertoire of the Le Corbusier-Jeanneret-Perriand furniture that Perriand compiled about 1938 indicates, moreover, that particular finishes were preferred for each of the various models (fig. 73). She noted, for example, that the chaise longue had a chrome frame and painted base, while the adjustable-back armchair was made in chrome, and the five-cushion "Grand Confort" armchair came in a lacquered finish. Her revolving chair could be upholstered in leather or caning, while the chaise could be had in a serviceable stretched fabric, pony, or calf.[17]

Mies van der Rohe's furniture was also available in a range of colors and upholstery. All of his models were made between 1927 and 1930 by the Berliner Metallgewerbe Joseph Müller, and, from 1931, most of them by an offshoot, the Bamberg Metallwerkstätten, both in Berlin. (Thonet also produced several models, which were included in its 1930–31 catalogue.) Bamberg, as indicated on its 1931 price list of designs by Mies and his close col-

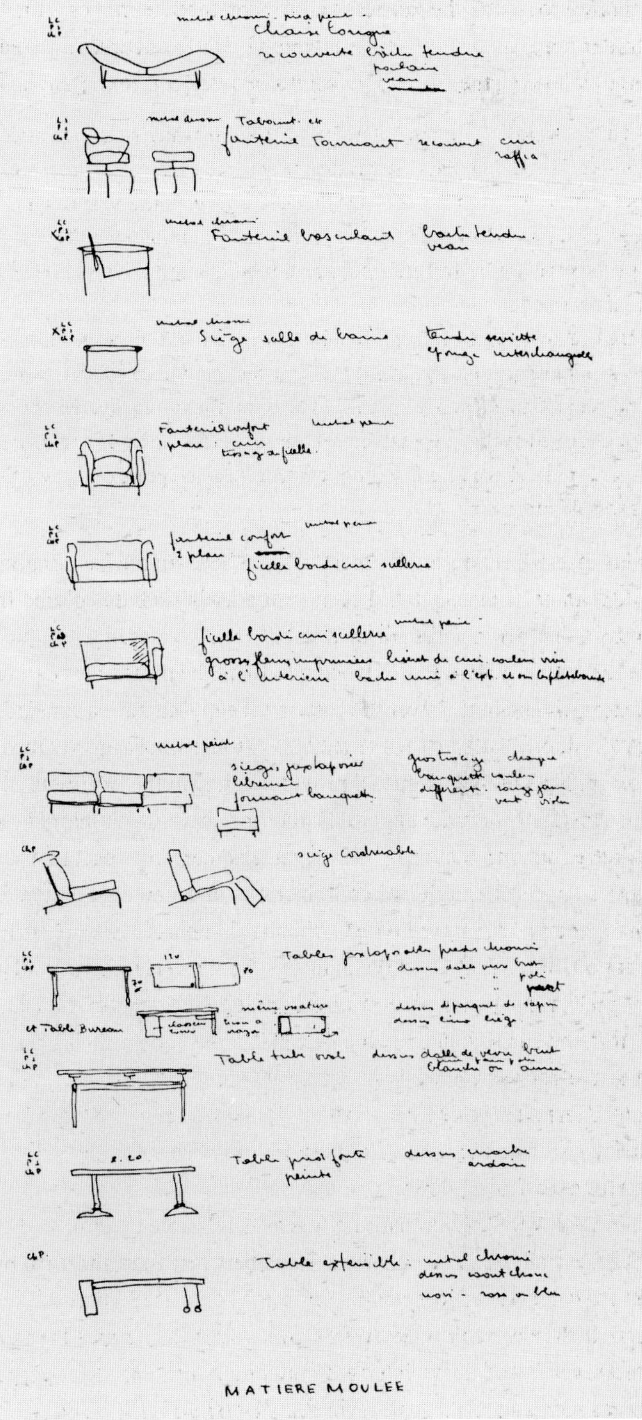

73 CHARLOTTE PERRIAND
Manuscript catalogue of the furniture of Le Corbusier, Pierre Jeanneret, and Charlotte Perriand, c. 1938.

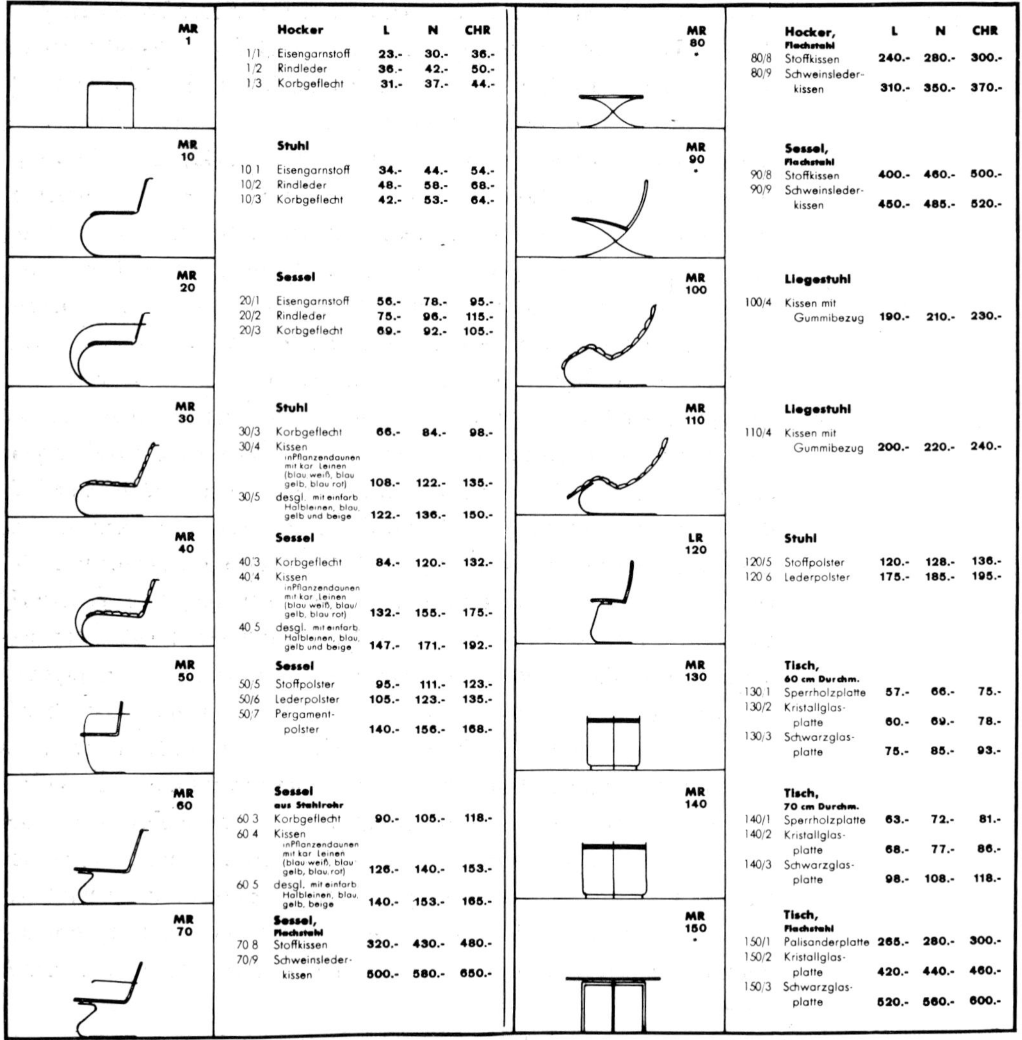

Modell	Nr.	Bezeichnung	L	N	CHR
MR 1		**Hocker**			
	1/1	Eisengarnstoff	23.-	30.-	36.-
	1/2	Rindleder	36.-	42.-	50.-
	1/3	Korbgeflecht	31.-	37.-	44.-
MR 10		**Stuhl**			
	10/1	Eisengarnstoff	34.-	44.-	54.-
	10/2	Rindleder	48.-	58.-	68.-
	10/3	Korbgeflecht	42.-	53.-	64.-
MR 20		**Sessel**			
	20/1	Eisengarnstoff	56.-	78.-	95.-
	20/2	Rindleder	75.-	96.-	115.-
	20/3	Korbgeflecht	69.-	92.-	105.-
MR 30		**Stuhl**			
	30/3	Korbgeflecht	66.-	84.-	98.-
	30/4	Kissen inPflanzendaunen mit kar. Leinen (blau weiß, blau gelb, blau rot)	108.-	122.-	135.-
	30/5	desgl. mit einfarb. Halbleinen, blau, gelb und beige	122.-	136.-	150.-
MR 40		**Sessel**			
	40/3	Korbgeflecht	84.-	120.-	132.-
	40/4	Kissen inPflanzendaunen mit kar. Leinen (blau weiß, blau/gelb, blau rot)	132.-	155.-	175.-
	40/5	desgl. mit einfarb. Halbleinen, blau, gelb und beige	147.-	171.-	192.-
MR 50		**Sessel**			
	50/5	Stoffpolster	95.-	111.-	123.-
	50/6	Lederpolster	105.-	123.-	135.-
	50/7	Pergamentpolster	140.-	156.-	168.-
MR 60		**Sessel aus Stahlrohr**			
	60/3	Korbgeflecht	90.-	105.-	118.-
	60/4	Kissen inPflanzendaunen mit kar. Leinen (blau weiß, blau gelb, blau, rot)	126.-	140.-	153.-
	60/5	desgl. mit einfarb. Halbleinen, blau, gelb, beige	140.-	153.-	165.-
MR 70		**Sessel, Flachstahl**			
	70/8	Stoffkissen	320.-	430.-	480.-
	70/9	Schweinslederkissen	500.-	580.-	650.-
MR 80 •		**Hocker, Flachstahl**			
	80/8	Stoffkissen	240.-	280.-	300.-
	80/9	Schweinslederkissen	310.-	350.-	370.-
MR 90 •		**Sessel, Flachstahl**			
	90/8	Stoffkissen	400.-	460.-	500.-
	90/9	Schweinslederkissen	450.-	485.-	520.-
MR 100		**Liegestuhl**			
	100/4	Kissen mit Gummibezug	190.-	210.-	230.-
MR 110		**Liegestuhl**			
	110/4	Kissen mit Gummibezug	200.-	220.-	240.-
LR 120		**Stuhl**			
	120/5	Stoffpolster	120.-	128.-	136.-
	120/6	Lederpolster	175.-	185.-	195.-
MR 130		**Tisch, 60 cm Durchm.**			
	130/1	Sperrholzplatte	57.-	66.-	75.-
	130/2	Kristallglasplatte	60.-	69.-	78.-
	130/3	Schwarzglasplatte	75.-	85.-	93.-
MR 140		**Tisch, 70 cm Durchm.**			
	140/1	Sperrholzplatte	63.-	72.-	81.-
	140/2	Kristallglasplatte	68.-	77.-	86.-
	140/3	Schwarzglasplatte	98.-	108.-	118.-
MR 150 •		**Tisch, Flachstahl**			
	150/1	Palisanderplatte	265.-	280.-	300.-
	150/2	Kristallglasplatte	420.-	440.-	460.-
	150/3	Schwarzglasplatte	520.-	560.-	600.-

74 Price list for metal furniture of Ludwig Mies van der Rohe and Lily Reich, Bamberg Metallwerkstätten, Berlin-Neukölln, 1931 (detail). Library of Congress, Washington, D.C., Mies van der Rohe Archive.

league Lily Reich (fig. 74), offered its metal frames in three finishes—nickel, chrome, and lacquer (yellow, red, and blue)—with the upholstery, depending on the model, in leather, caning, parchment, and fabric with similarly strong colors.

Unlike the production-oriented pieces of Breuer and the "types" of Le Corbusier that aimed to be universal, most of Mies's furniture was designed for a particular setting and its subsequent manufacture was individual, not on the scale of Thonet. Like his most impressive work, the chair for the German pavilion at the 1929 Exposición Internacional in Barcelona (colorplate 13), it was neither directed toward a mass market nor standardized for efficient production. The Barcelona pavilion (colorplate 14), a low steel-and-glass building with walls of marble, was as baroque a conception as Mies could have had considering the rigorous self-restraint of his craft. A temporary structure commissioned as an afterthought and erected very quickly (now rebuilt), it served simply as a ceremonial space where the king and queen of Spain would officially open the Weimar Republic's participation at the fair. To underscore this ceremonial function, Mies chose materials suited for royal reception rooms, alluding to the opulence of palatial decoration with richly colored and veined marbles—green for the walls on the exterior and a golden-brown onyx for the interior divider—and used white marble for the floor. To this palette, perhaps having been expected to introduce the red, black, and gold of the German flag, he added a deep red velvet curtain and a black woolen carpet on which he placed two ample shiny metal chairs upholstered in white kid leather. "In this context," Mies explained, "the Barcelona Chair could not be just a chair—it had to be a monumental object as well, but a monumental object which would not block the special flow of the building."[18] The original chairs were fabricated in Germany of flat, chromed, steel bars, and upholstered with the two large, horsehair cushions of loosely tufted pigskin "made by an old upholstery firm in Berlin—the finest craftsmen I could find" (fig. 75). Their form follows the X-shape of an elemental chair design that dates back to antiquity; their particular grace comes from the combination of the semi-circular sweep of the thin metal bar that seems to float free of the back cushions (which are supported by leather straps) and continues down to form the front leg, and the seat support, which mirrors this curve until the bars meet, and then bends back in an S-curve to form the back leg. For the Barcelona pavilion Mies also created matching stools and a trestle table of the same form.

For the house of the Tugendhat family in Brno, Czechoslovakia, in 1929–30 Mies designed two chairs, a comfortable armchair for the living room (fig. 76) and a compact dining chair (fig. 77), known respectively as the Tugendhat and Brno chairs. Both use the cantilever principle, but the Tugendhat design has an S-curved resilient base onto which the frame is screwed, giving it a somewhat awkward appearance. Both were made with tubular as well as flat bar frames, the former being used more often for the dining chair and the latter for the lounge chair. The interior of the Tugendhat house was particularly sumptuous, with its rich coloration, chosen with the assistance of Lily Reich,[19] carried over from the Barcelona pavilion. The living room was furnished with emerald green leather "Barcelona" chairs, silver gray upholstered "Tugendhat" chairs, and a ruby red velvet reclining chair,[20] a palette as out of keeping with what we customarily visualize as a functionalist

75 LUDWIG MIES VAN DER ROHE
German pavilion, Exposición Internacional, Barcelona, 1929.
The Museum of Modern Art, New York, Mies van der Rohe Archive.

76 LUDWIG MIES VAN DER ROHE
Living room of Tugendhat house, Brno, Czechoslovakia, 1929–30. The Museum of Modern Art, New York, Mies van der Rohe Archive.

77 LUDWIG MIES VAN DER ROHE
Dining room of Tugendhat house, Brno, Czechoslovakia, 1929–30. The Museum of Modern Art, New York, Mies van der Rohe Archive.

interior as that of the canary yellow leather "Barcelona" chair that Philip Johnson recalled seeing in 1930 in an apartment Mies designed in Berlin.[21]

Of all the numerous models of tubular-steel furniture manufactured during the 1920s and 1930s, the designs of Marcel Breuer, the Le Corbusier group, and Mies van der Rohe are the ones that are most widely in production today. Their popularity in the postwar period, the result of circumstances distinct from those of their initial reception, should not suggest that they had achieved comparable success earlier, or that success had come easily. Business relations were vexed, and the quality was not always what the designers would have liked, for manufacturing processes were evolving and production standards were not consistently maintained. This was especially a problem with Thonet because the company produced large quantities of furniture by licensing their models to factories in different countries. As early as 1930 Le Corbusier, Jeanneret, and Perriand were expressing their concern to Thonet over licensing and royalties,[22] and by 1934 Le Corbusier was fully outraged over the broad dissemination of their furniture, for which he claimed he never received compensation. He took the opportunity of responding to an invitation from the Thonet licensee in Czechoslovakia, Mücke-Melder Werke, to explain his position: "I am very seriously disappointed by the issue concerning the exploitation of the models of our furniture. I came to an agreement with M. THONET for the sale of my models in France and abroad. The results that are reported to me periodically by the THONET office are all terrible. So terrible that I have to admit that my models are not meeting with success. Is it true or isn't it? I am not sure. You told me you were a licensee of THONET. Would you perhaps be so kind as to let me know if our models are delivered by you or sold by you in a regular & lucrative fashion."[23] Le Corbusier could not have been very happy when he received the answer, for he was told point-blank that his works were not doing well, and that in general people preferred the models of Mart Stam.[24]

By the end of the 1930s production of metal furniture had declined. Under the threat of conflict, vernacular styles considered patriotic emerged. In Germany under the Nazi regime, metal furniture was deemed unsuited for the home, although it was accepted for commercial uses, and in Great Britain, as soon as the war began, the Utility program prescribed wood furniture based on Arts and Crafts principles. Wartime restrictions on the use of critical resources put an end to the manufacture of metal furniture just as it was being reinvigorated as the dinette set in the United States, where, after the war, it would achieve the truly popular market to which its originator had aspired (fig. 78).

78 Advertisement for Howell "Chromsteel" dinette set, 1946. From *House Beautiful* (February 1946). The New York Public Library.

NEW *Beauty and Charm*

COME INTO YOUR KITCHEN AND DINETTE

Here is gay, sparkling furniture that brings new beauty and charm into your kitchen and dinette . . . it's the kind that seems to stay new looking indefinitely.

From many table designs you can choose the exact Chromsteel* kitchen or dinette set you have been wanting. Some tables have Plastex* tops in handsome colors that are chip-proof and heat-resisting. Others have beautiful natural Birchwood tops. Most tables extend or have leaves that pull out . . . to provide extra space quickly. Howell tubular Chromsteel chairs to match are really comfortable and practically wear-proof . . . some have rich Fabrikoid* upholstery . . . others colorful baked enamel on seats and backs.

Leading furniture and department stores display and sell Howell Chromsteel Furniture . . . the Howell trademark identifies the genuine. For full-color booklet and name of the dealer near you . . . write The Howell Company, St. Charles, Illinois.

*TRADE-MARK

Genuine HOWELL ST. CHARLES, ILLINOIS Chromsteel

THE LABEL TO LOOK FOR

1 Marcel Breuer, "Metallmöbel und moderne Räumlichkeit," *Das Neue Frankfurt*, January 1928, p. 11; translated as "Metal Furniture and Modern Accommodation," in Württembergischer Kunstverein, Stuttgart, *50 Years Bauhaus* (1968), p. 109.

2 John Gloag, "Wood or Metal?" *The Studio* 97 (1929), pp. 49–50; Charlotte Perriand, "Wood or Metal?" *The Studio* 97 (1929), pp. 278–79.

3 Werner Möller and Otakar Máčel, *Ein Stuhl macht Geschichte* (Munich: Prestel, 1992).

4 Ludwig Mies van der Rohe, response to questionnaire sent by Nikolaus Pevsner, 1935; quoted in Ludwig Glaeser, *Ludwig Mies van der Rohe: Furniture and Furniture Drawings from the Design Collection and the Mies van der Rohe Archive* (New York: The Museum of Modern Art, 1977), p. 9.

5 Mart Stam, "De stoel gedurende de laatste 40 jaar," in *8 & Opbouw* (1935), p. 7; quoted in Jan van Geest and Otakar Máčel, *Stühle aus Stahl: Metallmöbel 1925–1940* (Cologne: Verlag der Buchhandlung Walther König, 1980), p. 47.

6 Marcel Valotaire, "The Paris Salons," *The Studio* 96 (1928), p. 203.

7 H.-A. Martinie, "Le XVIIIe Salon des Artistes Décorateurs," *Art et Décoration* 53 (June 1928), pp. 165, 166.

8 See Akio Izutsu, *The Bauhaus: A Japanese Perspective and a Profile of Hans and Florence Schust Knoll* (Tokyo: Kajima Institute Publishing Company, 1992), pp. 44–47.

9 See Oliver Thorne, "The Modern Metal Chair," *Home & Field* 40 (May 1930), pp. 50–55.

10 See Christopher Wilk, *Thonet: 150 Years of Furniture* (Woodbury, N. Y., and London: Barron's, 1980), pp. 98–111.

11 See *Thonet Stahlrohrmöbel: Steckkartenkatalog* (Thonet Tubular Steel Furniture: Card Catalogue), facsimile reprint of 1930–31 packet of loose cards showing the complete line of Thonet metal furniture (Weil am Rhein, Germany: Vitra Design Museum, 1989).

12 "Charlotte Perriand Looks Back (and Forward)" [interview], *Architectural Review* 176 (November 1984), pp. 65–66.

13 Le Corbusier, "The Undertaking of Furniture" [1929], in *Precisions on the Present State of Architecture and City Planning* (Cambridge, Mass., and London: The MIT Press, 1991), p. 118.

14 Martinie, "XVIIIe Salon," p. 168.

15 *Thonet Stahlrohrmöbel: Steckkartenkatalog.*

16 Perriand, "Wood or Metal?" p. 279.

17 See Arthur Rüegg, "Anmerkungen zum *Equipement de l'habitation* und zur *Polychromie intérieure* bei Le Corbusier," in Villa Malpensata, Lugano, *Le Corbusier: la ricerca paziente* (1980), pp. 151–61.

18 Mies van der Rohe to I. D. Higgins, Leeds, England, January 2, 1964, Ludwig Mies van der Rohe Archive, Library of Congress, Washington, D. C., Container 28, Furniture.

19 See Glaeser, *Ludwig Mies van der Rohe*, p. 10.

20 Ibid.

21 "Epilogue: Thirty Years After" [discussion], in Philip C. Johnson, *Mies van der Rohe*, 3rd ed., rev. (New York: The Museum of Modern Art, 1978), p. 205.

22 As indicated in Thonet Frères to Le Corbusier, P. Jeanneret, & Ch. Perriand, Paris, July 7, 1930, Le Corbusier Archives, Fondation Le Corbusier, Paris, F 1 (3) Meubles, doc. 33; and Le Corbusier to Bruno Weill, director, Thonet, November 21, 1931, doc. 174.

23 Le Corbusier to Mücke-Melder Werke, Fryštát, Czechoslovakia, May 9, 1935, in ibid., doc. 177.

24 Mücke-Melder Werke to Le Corbusier, May 14, 1935, in ibid., doc. 178.

Machine Art

Whether the movement be called "functionalism,"
"modernism," "sachlichkeit," "stile razionale," "international
style," or "machine art," the style is uniform
and is easily recognizable in the objects themselves.

Philip Johnson[1]

Functionalist design was shepherded to the United States by the Museum of Modern Art in New York. Devoid of any lingering utilitarian or social pretenses, it arrived full-blown as a style, which the museum contrived to provide with a coherent aesthetic that would bring it into line with the purist European artistic movements it promulgated. While design had been shown by the museum almost from its founding in 1929, and the museum had also presented an influential review of contemporary architecture in its International Style exhibition in 1932, the aesthetic that brought functionalist design wholly within the museum's clutches was not devised until 1934, when it opened the exhibition entitled "Machine Art," organized by Philip Johnson, the museum's director of architecture.[2]

"The objects in the exhibition," the museum's invitation to its members explained, "are produced by machines for domestic, commercial, industrial and scientific purposes. Beauty—mathematical, mechanical and utilitarian—determined the choice of the objects regardless of whether their fine design was intended by artist or engineer, or merely a concomitant of machine production."[3] The exhibition joined machinery and machine parts, standardized products, and furniture and appliances—allegedly but in actuality not always—made by machine, mostly in America. In line with the prevalent style of the 1930s in Europe for presenting modern products, everything looked cool, shiny, and abundant (fig. 79), an American realization of the Werkbund's advertising for its Stuttgart exhibition in 1924 (fig. 21) and its installation at the Paris Salon in 1930 (fig. 80).

The "Machine Art" show was not the first time that machinery and manufactured objects had appeared in the United States in an art gallery or exhibition, but it was the first instance in which they were shown independently, without reference to the other arts. An early predecessor, the "Machine-Age Exposition" held in New York in 1927, had presented machines and mechanical elements (including motors, valves, meters, gears, ball bearings, a propeller, coffee grinders, and a crank shaft) along with architectural photo-

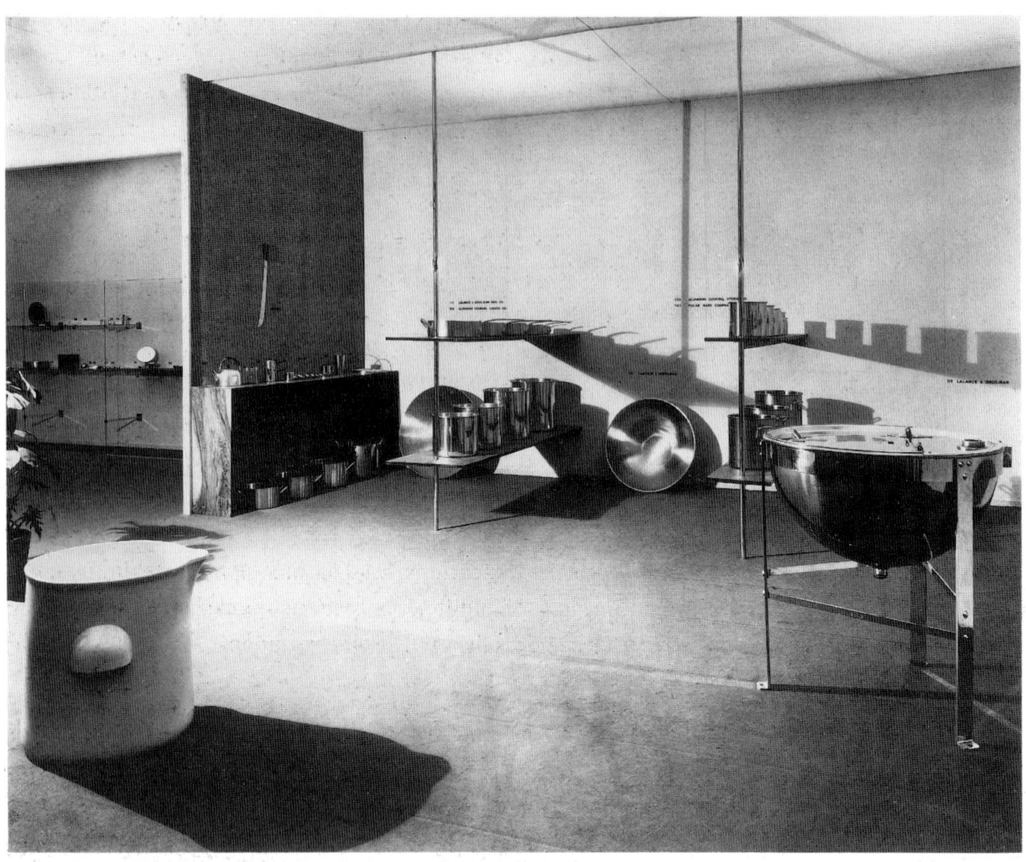

79 PHILIP JOHNSON
"Machine Art," The Museum of Modern Art, New York, 1934.

graphs, sculpture, handmade silver, stained glass, paintings, and constructions as an homage to "a great new race of men in America: the engineer. He has created a new mechanical world," reported the supplement to the *Little Review*, which served as the catalogue, its cover featuring a mechanistic design by Fernand Léger (fig. 82). "It is inevitable and important for the civilization of today that he make a union with the architect and artist. . . . The men who hold first rank in the plastic arts today are the men who are organizing and transforming the realities of our age into a dynamic beauty. They do not copy or imitate the Machine, they do not worship the Machine,—They recognize it as one of the realities."[4]

Although the Museum of Modern Art wrote off the "Machine-Age Exposition" as an "important pioneer effort," but one in which the "romantic attitude toward the machine reached its height in America,"[5] "Machine Art" was not so far from it, only more exclusive. Seeking to demonstrate that the aesthetic base of modernism could be applied to engineered products, it was an attempt to establish standards for machine-made objects based on "eternal" forms as well as a polemic against pragmatic styling, streamlining, and geometric Moderne decoration, which were then vying for primacy in product design in America. How this aesthetic should be defined was suggested in the foreword to the catalogue by the museum's director, Alfred H. Barr, Jr. "The beauty of machine art," he declared, "is in part the abstract beauty of 'straight lines and circles' made into actual tangible 'surfaces and solids' by means of tools, 'lathes and rulers and squares.' In Plato's day the tools were simple handworker's implements but today, as a result of the perfection of modern materials and the precision of modern instruments, the modern machine-made object approaches far more closely and more frequently those pure shapes the contemplation of which Plato calls the first of the 'pure pleasures.'" If geometry was the ideal, following Le Corbusier as well as Plato, and the link between the machine and Machine Art, "perfection of surface" was an indication of its quality. This, Barr said, "is, of course, made possible by the refinement of modern materials and the precision of machine manufacture. A watch spring is beautiful not only for its spiral shape but also for its bright steel surface and its delicately exact execution." An acute selectivity

80 HERBERT BAYER "German Section," installation at the Exposition de la Société des Artistes Décorateurs, Grand Palais, Paris, 1930. From *Form* (1930).

was required, however, if the machine was to become the basis for a design aesthetic in this sense, for not all machine products would do: "A watch crystal, perfect though it may be," Barr continued, "is too simple a form to hold our visual interest for long. A printing press, on the other hand, is too complicated an arrangement of shapes for the human eye to enjoy aesthetically. Moderately simple machine compositions such as the door of a wall safe or the microscope or our classical example, the ball bearing [fig. 81] prove more satisfactory."

Reactions to the show were mixed (fig. 83). Henry McBride, art critic for the *New York Sun,* claimed that "there can be no infinitesimal trace of art in an object made by machinery. That is not what art is";[6] while *The New Yorker*, in a smug response, reported coming away "a little dazed.... It's disturbing,

81 SVEN WINGQUIST Self-aligning ball bearing, 1929. Made by SKF Industries, Inc. Chrome-plated steel. Diameter 8½" (21.6 cm). The Museum of Modern Art, New York. Gift of the manufacturer.

82 *Machine-Age Exposition*, supplement to *Little Review* (1927).

after all, to discover that you've been surrounded by beauty all your life and have never known it."[7] The critic for the *New York Evening Post* easily pointed out the flaw in the museum's manipulation of utility and art:

> If a functionalist, one should consider anything beautiful which works with the utmost efficiency to its designated end. Therefore, the functionalist should not be thrilled by the fact that a cross-section of a wire rope makes a handsome geometrical pattern, or that by wresting springs out of their natural environment in a typewriter a pretty design of concentric loops may be effected.... True, if you take any of these objects apart, their wheels, cylinders, lenses and other mechanical detail prove to have engaging geometrical patterns, especially when displayed separately. But such dissection destroys the purpose for which they were created and consequently invalidates their existence.[8]

By showing machines and mechanical elements as art (fig. 84), independent of but allied to the mechanistic imagery of a whole category of works in other divisions of its collection, the Museum of Modern Art held up these carefully selected examples as the basis of a new concrete aesthetic, Machine Art, and as the visual model for design. "Machine Art is not only produced by the machine," the museum's *Bulletin* noted in 1933, "but its design is inspired by the machine. It is logical that a machine will have its greatest success in creating in its own image."[9] This statement follows Le Corbusier directly: "Machines beget machines. They are now abundant, and they can be seen gleaming everywhere. Their polish is on the sections. The sections reveal the geometry that controls everything. If we polish the sections, it is to reach for their functional perfection."[10] Machine Art interpreted the machine in black and white, as it might have been known from illustrations in magazines or in Le Corbusier's books, isolated, austere, and colorless, through the cool monochromatic vision of the American Precisionist painter Charles Sheeler rather than the frenetic, coloristic interpretation of the Frenchman Léger. But in reading Le Corbusier, the organizers ignored the architect's own description of the machines that he ennobled: "The machines are adorned with colour, with grey, with vermilion, with green, with blue. Grey on the complex castings, bright colours on the pure geometry of the sections."[11] Léger described the machines of his day in much the same way: "Each machine-object has two material qualities: a constant surface, often painted which absorbs light (architectural value); another surface, most often of white metal, which reflects light and takes the role of unlimited imagination (painterly value).... We are currently facing an unprecedented invasion of the multicoloured useful object. Even the agricultural machine is becoming pleasant in character, garbed like a butterfly or a bird."[12]

If "Machine Art" narrowed the aesthetic of functionalism through its emphasis on formalism and neutrality, it also misrepresented the mode of pro-

83 Cartoon by Alain: "Recognition at last! The Museum of Modern Art wants to give me a one-man show." From *The New Yorker* (April 14, 1934).

duction of the works exhibited. From the very beginning, the museum had problems with machine manufacture because many of the objects that met the formalist criteria and were included in the exhibition had not in fact been made by machine. The story is told of how Philip Johnson insisted on including a meerschaum pipe made by the British tobacconist Dunhill (possibly because of its strong associations with Le Corbusier, who illustrated a similar pipe as the final plate in his book *Towards a New Architecture*[13]), but the company, which was rightfully proud of its handmade merchandise, objected. It took the intervention of Nelson Rockefeller, a museum trustee and landlord of Dunhill's shop in Rockefeller Center, to get the firm's agreement on including the pipe in the exhibition.[14] The metal furniture that was exhibited belonged to a group of works whose fabrication was essentially a hand operation, and even for a firm like Thonet, whose standardized production by industrial methods reached substantial levels, the intervention of machinery was minimal once the metal tubing was prepared. This is demonstrated by a photograph of a workman in a German factory about 1930 bending a piece of metal furniture into shape (fig. 85).

The museum insisted on tying the "look" associated with the machine to the processes of machine manufacture instead of accepting the fact that

84 PHILIP JOHNSON
"Machine Art," The Museum of Modern Art, New York, 1934.

this aesthetic was an homage to an idea, not an actual practice. Lewis Mumford saw the issue more clearly in his book *Technics and Civilization*:

> In creating the machine, we have set before ourselves a positively inhuman standard of perfection. No matter what the occasion, the criterion of successful mechanical form is that it should look *as if* no human hand had touched it. In that effort, in that boast, in that achievement the human hand shows itself, perhaps, in its most cunning manifestation. And yet ultimately it is to the human organism that we must return to achieve the final touch of perfection. . . . Very frequently, in machine work, the best structure is forfeited to the mere conveniences of production: given equally high standards of performance, the machine can often no more than hold its own in competition with the hand product. The pinnacles of handicraft art set a standard that the machine must constantly hold before it.[15]

Through the idea of Machine Art, the Museum of Modern Art established its own set of requirements for design—an aesthetic (simplicity, purity, geometry, and also austerity), a method of production (machine manufacture, actual or implied, using modern materials), and an iconography (the machine, as selectively defined)—which it construed as functionalism. This was embraced as the guiding spirit of the museum's design collection, and over the next years the institution became virtually unyielding in the vehemence with which it held to the concept of Machine Art. Because of the museum's position as the only art institution seriously collecting, exhibiting, and publishing industrial design, its philosophy became the standard for those who were concerned with the aesthetics of this field. Considering the centrality of this concept to the museum's design activities and the impact it would have internationally, Johnson's account of the genesis of Machine Art seems peculiarly offhand. "[We coined the term] while we were drinking," he recounted. "It was about 4:00 in the morning, and the words 'machine art' just came out of the air, a very, very good idea. Funny that it doesn't seem like an idea anymore, it's just machine art, but in those days it was an invention from the air. So, that made it very, very easy because we could find the objects all the way from non-designed things—pots and pans—and then we tried to find objects that were designed by names, and there hardly were any names, so we felt we'd better stress just the very fact of the beauty of the objects that were just the result of other forces than design."[16]

While most of the objects in the exhibition had been made in America, it was to Germany that Johnson looked for the source of Machine Art, "particu-

85 Workman manufacturing tubular-steel furniture, c. 1930. From Erich Dieckmann, *Möbelbau in Holz, Rohr und Stahl* (Stuttgart, 1931).

larly," as he wrote in the catalogue, its "post-war generation [which] prided itself on achieving a mechanistic age and on designing the proper utensils for living in it. This was most clearly expressed in the Bauhaus."[17] Among the few foreign examples in the exhibition were two works by Marcel Breuer, his nesting tables (although unattributed) and his cantilever side chair, and one by the Le Corbusier-Jeanneret-Perriand team, their armchair with an adjustable back. The museum was already acquiring tubular-metal furniture by the French team (fig. 72) and by Ludwig Mies van der Rohe—probably the first in any public art museum—and had included such work in an exhibition in 1933, "Objects: 1900 and Today," which compared the principles of contemporary design with those of Art Nouveau.

The Museum of Modern Art aligned itself even more specifically with the Bauhaus through an exhibition in 1938 devoted to the program and work of the school under Walter Gropius, from 1919 to 1928.[18] The stylistic uniformity that could be seen among the products of the Bauhaus in the exhibition, antithetical as it was to the school's philosophy, was acknowledged and explained in the catalogue with an apologia by Gropius:

> notwithstanding individual differences among the collaborators, bauhaus products had a certain similarity in appearance, as may be seen in this book. this was not the result of following slavishly a stylized esthetic convention, since it was against just such imitativeness that the bauhaus revolted. it was the outcome of a unified conception of art developed by all the workers in common. at the same time, however, it was necessary to combat imitators and unintelligent admirers who thought that every unornamented building or implement was derived from the bauhaus "style" and who thus threatened to cheapen the meaning of bauhaus work. expressly stated: the goal of the bauhaus is not a "style," system, dogma, canon, recipe or fashion.[19]

Yet this disclaimer was belied right on the page by the catalogue's adoption of the Bauhaus typographic mannerism of eliminating capital letters from its publications, which had determined the format of this passage when it was first published in 1930.

Complaints of a style particular to the Bauhaus had appeared as early as its first exhibition in 1923, and continued throughout its existence.[20] In 1930 Ernst Kállai, a supporter of Hannes Meyer, who had just been forced to resign as director of the Bauhaus, wrote an insightful critique of the apparent paradox in theory and practice broached by Gropius:

> It cannot be denied, however, that the work of the Bauhaus itself is in no way free of esthetic overcultivation and dangerous formalism. It is true that discarding all ornamentation and banning each and every curved plane and line in the design of houses, furniture, and appliances has led to the creation of very interesting, new,

> and simple forms. But whatever was obvious about these new functional forms has by no means always made as much sense. Rather, the products which were to be expedient and functional, technical and constructive, and economically necessary were for the most part conceived out of a taste-oriented arbitrariness decked out in new clothes, and out of a *bel-esprit* propensity for elementary geometric configurations and for the formal characteristics of technical contrivances. Art and technology, the new unity—this is what it was theoretically called and accordingly practiced—interested in technology, but art-directed. This is a critical "but." Priority was given to the art-directedness. There was the new formalistic willfulness, the desire to create a style at all costs, and technology had to yield to this conviction.[21]

Disregarding the similarities that must have been apparent in the works in the exhibition, as well as previous criticism of the Bauhaus, the reviewer for *The Art Digest* could still take Gropius at his word, stating that "strangely, and yet in perfect accord with Gropius' founding principle, the Bauhaus alone of all 'art movements' of the 20th century, did not develop a style. There is no such thing as *Bauhausism*."[22]

Notes

1 Philip Johnson, "Architecture and Industrial Art," in Alfred H. Barr, Jr., ed., *Modern Works of Art* (New York: The Museum of Modern Art and W. W. Norton and Company, 1934), p. 20.

2 See Philip Johnson, *Machine Art* (New York: The Museum of Modern Art and W. W. Norton and Company, 1934); see also Sidney Lawrence, "Clean Machines at the Modern," *Art in America* 72 (February 1984), pp. 127–41, 166–68; and Terry Smith, *Making the Modern: Industry, Art, and Design in America* (Chicago and London: The University of Chicago Press, 1993), pp. 385–401.

3 "Machine Art" members invitation, The Museum of Modern Art, New York, 1934, The Museum of Modern Art, New York, Archive pamphlet file, MOMA 34 Machine Art.

4 Jane Heap, in *Machine-Age Exposition*, supplement to *Little Review* 11 (1927), p. 36.

5 Alfred H. Barr, Jr., Foreword, in Johnson, *Machine Art*, n.p. The following quotations are also from this unpaginated catalogue.

6 Henry McBride [review], *New York Sun*, March 10, 1934.

7 Talk of the Town, *The New Yorker*, March 17, 1934, p. 18.

8 Margaret Breuning, "Modern Museum Puts on Machine Art Exhibit," *New York Evening Post*, March 10, 1934.

9 *The Bulletin of the Museum of Modern Art* 1 (November 1, 1933), n.p.

10 Le Corbusier, *The Decorative Art of Today*, translated by James I. Dunnett (Cambridge, Mass.: The MIT Press, 1987), p. 112.

11 Ibid.

12 Fernand Léger, "The Machine Aesthetic: The Manufactured Object, the Artisan and the Artist" [1924]; translated in The Tate Gallery, London, *Léger and Purist Paris* (1970), pp. 88, 89.

13 Le Corbusier, *Towards a New Architecture*, translated by Frederick Etchells (London: John Rodker Publisher, 1927), p. 289.

14 See Richard Guy Wilson, "Machine Aesthetics," in Richard Guy Wilson, Dianne H.

Pilgrim, and Dickran Tashjian, *The Machine Age in America, 1918–1941* (New York: The Brooklyn Museum in association with Harry N. Abrams Publishers, 1986), p. 53.

15 Lewis Mumford, *Technics and Civilization* (New York: Harcourt, Brace and Company, 1934), pp. 358–59.

16 Philip Johnson [interviewed by Sharon Zane], The Museum of Modern Art Oral History Project, December 1990, January, February, 1991, pp. 52–53, The Museum of Modern Art, New York, Archives.

17 Philip Johnson, "History of Machine Art," in *Machine Art*, n. p.

18 Organized in collaboration with Gropius and his wife Ise, who along with Herbert Bayer edited the accompanying book, *Bauhaus, 1919–1928* (New York: The Museum of Modern Art, 1938).

19 Ibid., p. 206; this had been first published in Walter Gropius, *Bauhausbauten Dessau* (Dessau: Bauhaus, 1930).

20 See Sigrid Wortmann Weltge, *Women's Work: Textile Art from the Bauhaus* (San Francisco: Chronicle Books, 1993), p. 185.

21 Ernst Kállai, *Die Weltbühne*, no. 21 (January 1930); translated as "Ten Years of Bauhaus," in Hans M. Wingler, *The Bauhaus: Weimar Dessau Berlin Chicago* (Cambridge, Mass., and London: The MIT Press, 1969), p. 162.

22 "Modern Museum Illustrates the Bauhaus Idea," *The Art Digest* 13 (December 15, 1938), p. 6.

The Bauhaus Style

It is high time that we stop using the cliché "Bauhaus style,"
which only ignorance of the most elementary facts
of the twenties could have allowed to become current.

Walter Dexel (Bauhaus student)[1]

The 1960s witnessed the triumph of functionalist design, implemented with considerably greater visibility and impact than it had during the 1920s. By now familiarly called the Bauhaus Style and codified in a full lexicon of techniques and materials, it became the accepted mode for civic and corporate buildings and their furnishings, especially in the United States. Viewed then simply as a continuation of the movement that had originated in Germany before the Nazi takeover and the interruption of World War II, this second flowering actually differed from the original, and had many of the contradictions that revivals seem to exhibit. The confusion was understandable because a number of the German functionalist architects and designers, now residing in America, were at its helm, and the new functionalism encompassed a subtle rewriting of history as their earlier works were reproduced three decades later, in new materials and with new technologies, according to a revised aesthetic that met the expectations of the materialist postwar era. The artifacts of this revival, now managed completely on a corporate level, were reeditions or copies of functionalist designs of the 1920s (none of the original furniture remained in industrial production after the war); new works created in a doctrinaire functionalist mode; and stylistic pastiches, such as

86 "Corbu," "Wassily," and "New Bauhaus" armchairs, c. 1965. From *Stendig Index, Lounge Seating* (1970).

168 CORBU

1925 WASSILY

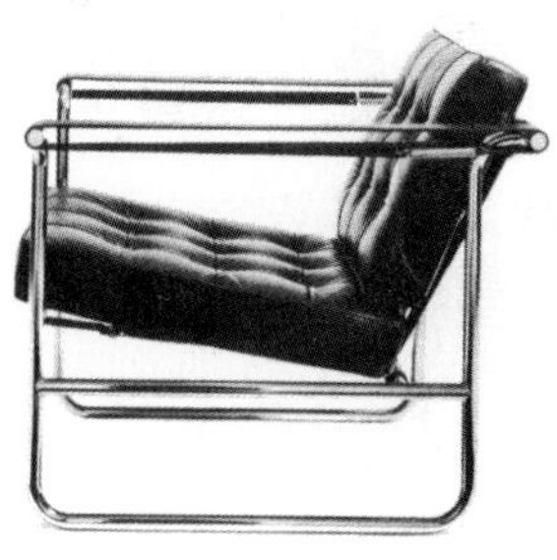

122 NEW BAUHAUS

the hybrid "New Bauhaus" armchair illustrated alongside two representatives of the style that inspired it in a catalogue of the American furniture company Stendig (fig. 86). This armchair has as dubious a relation to the spirit of its sources as Renaissance- or Rococo-revival pieces of the nineteenth century had to theirs. Functionalism was coopted by the fame of the Bauhaus; regardless of historical truth, the Bauhaus was given precedence over other expressions of the aesthetic, and the ideas and output of the school—and its very name—were conflated with the history of functionalism itself.

An attempt to revive the teaching of functionalism through a successor to the Bauhaus was undertaken in 1953 at the Hochschule für Gestaltung in Ulm, West Germany, under the direction of Max Bill, a painter and sculptor who had studied at the school in Dessau from 1927 to 1929. Rekindling its bold aspirations to revive civilization with the tools of design, and reintroducing aspects of the theory and the practice of the Bauhaus, most notably its influential preliminary course, Bill continued to emphasize the Werkbund ideals of form and beauty, which were the underlying goals of his own work (fig. 1) and the subject of an exhibition entitled "Die Gute Form" that Bill himself had organized for the Schweizer Werkbund in 1949.[2] The old Bauhaus goal of providing research for industry, revived at Ulm, had its most remarkable success during the 1950s in a collaboration with the German appliance manufacturer Braun, which, adopting the functionalist vocabulary at first, developed the concept of product families, now accepted throughout the trade. The relevance of aesthetic- and form-based design was later questioned, however, as practical needs, such as harnessing technology, became more insistent, and design at Ulm after Bill left was directed away from discrete objects and the leftover vocabulary of stylistic functionalism to systems and planning, incorporating mathematics and the sciences more and more into its working method. Hans Roericht's institutional stacking china, a thesis project at Ulm in 1959 based on extensive research of utility and manufacture (fig. 87), brought systematic planning and new forms to tableware design, utilizing for efficiency's sake the anonymity and repetition that was earlier a distinctive stylistic trait of functionalist designers (fig. 28). Across the Atlantic, another bearer of the torch, the New Bauhaus—founded in Chicago in 1937 with the former Bauhaus master Lázsló Moholy-Nagy as director, and restructured in 1939 as the School (later Institute) of Design—likewise favored a Bauhaus-derived preliminary course but rejected the trappings of a functionalist style for a greater responsiveness to postwar technology and popular organic forms.

The late 1940s and 1950s embraced an expressionism and organicism in design that emphasized craft or craftlike production from natural materials, as well as the use of new, man-made substances and techniques that had been

87 HANS ROERICHT
Stacking table service, 1959. Made by Thomas Porzellan-Werke, Waldershof/Oberpfalz, Germany. Glazed porcelain. Height of coffeepot 8 1/8″ (20.5 cm). Die Neue Sammlung, Munich.

perfected during the war. The organic, biomorphic style drew on forms introduced in Scandinavia in the 1930s by such designers as Alvar Aalto and developed in the United States in the work of Isamu Noguchi and Russel Wright. Scandinavian "modern," oiled-wood furniture in gently flowing lines became the first postwar style to take hold internationally, and its tenacity on commercial interior design has remnants even today. Other directions as diverse as the baroque, laminated-wood desks and tables of Carlo Mollino in Italy and, in the United States, the molded plywood and plastic chairs of Charles Eames and Eero Saarinen, the quirky creations of George Nelson, and the free-form tables of Noguchi and their popular kidney-shaped derivatives diverted attention from the prewar fascination with both ascetic formalism and streamlining in metal and glass.[3]

There was little indication at the end of the war that functionalism would make a strong comeback. In 1950, writing in the *Magazine of Art*, Kay Fisker, himself a designer of notable machine-style objects (fig. 27) and buildings that had depended on the precepts of functionalism, looked around Europe and pronounced it dead:

> Functionalism was a cleansing agent which swept over the nations like a storm, liberating and stimulating. It was necessary, but it destroyed too much. Architecture became skeletal, sterile and antiseptic. At times the whole movement seemed inhuman. Reaction grew . . . a spontaneous reaction throughout the world against the penurious, the puristic and the over simplified. . . . The war has shaken many of us so fundamentally that it seems impossible to pick up the thread from the remote prehistoric days of 1939. Catastrophe has left us uncertain and suspicious; we no longer know in what to believe. . . . Those very architects who formerly helped to promote functionalism are now searching for other ideals.[4]

The way for a return of functionalism was not unprepared, however, for on an intellectual and theoretical level a band of committed historians, critics, and curators kept its values before their colleagues and the public. In 1947 the Museum of Modern Art organized the first retrospective exhibition of the work of Mies van der Rohe with a catalogue by Philip Johnson.[5] In 1949 the museum took an even more crucial step toward maintaining the aesthetic primacy of functionalism by issuing the second edition of Nikolaus Pevsner's treatise on design under the new title *Pioneers of Modern Design*. In Italy, in 1951, Giulio Carlo Argan published an extensive study of Walter Gropius and the Bauhaus,[6] the first reassessment to appear after the war. Three years later, a large exhibition, "Gropius and the Bauhaus," was held at the Tokyo National Museum of Modern Art. This exhibition underscored the reverence given the Bauhaus in Japan (and felt even now), which had been expressed earlier by the Japanese designers and architects who had studied at the school in the late 1920s and 1930s, and Gropius himself announced on his visit there that such an exhibition would have been "totally impossible to hold today in America or any European country."[7]

In 1957, Edward Robert De Zurko traced the theoretical antecedents of functionalism in his *Origins of Functionalist Theory*, first undertaken for a doctoral thesis at Columbia University. "Functionalism is in our midst," he reported. "Scarcely a month passes without the publication of some article in one of the architectural periodicals containing critical remarks, pro and con, pertaining to functionalism. It seems likely that a general idea, such as functionalism, which permits a variety of individual interpretations, will continue to inspire men.... The problem is to interpret functionalism broadly, so that it will inspire rather than restrict its protagonists and provide a sound basis for worthy creative expression."[8] This was not to be the case, however, for its resurrection in the United States followed a narrow, conservative, historicizing path rather than a broad and adventuresome one.

Americans who supported functionalism but had become disillusioned with European values after two successive conflicts abroad began to search out roots for the concept at home. With the publication in 1947 of a collection of essays on aesthetics by the nineteenth-century sculptor Horatio Greenough under the title *Form and Function*,[9] an American precedent was brought to light. The introduction by Erle Loran, a critic for *Art News* and an abstract painter, depicted Greenough's ideas as a significant precursor to functionalism and presented his work as a polemic for its American origins. To support this Loran cited such assertions of Greenough's as "Beauty is the promise of Function" and "embellishment [is] false beauty" (quoting, as well, Walt Whitman's parallel sentiment, from the introduction to *Leaves of Grass*, that "most works are most beautiful without ornament").

Loran also suggested that the sculptor's "desire to see working normal schools of structure and ornament, constantly occupied in designing for the manufacturers" was "not unlike that of the pre-Nazi German Bauhaus." But he lamented: "The lesson of Greenough has yet to be learned, especially by many architects who still hold power. What a bitter pill it should be for them to know that they are at least a hundred years behind the times, by standards set up by one of our own good ancestors in America! Instead of putting up resistance to the innovations of the European International School, with its 'machines for living,' and to the boldness and rashness of Frank Lloyd Wright, they might all this time have turned their fury against the farseeing Horatio Greenough."[10] Joseph Hudnut, dean of the faculty of design at Harvard University, agreed: "How condescending we have grown to our ancestors. How wholesome it is and how refreshing to see our most cherished ideas, after we have struggled to lay them before the world, set forth with such clarity and eloquence. There were ... great critics before Le Corbusier, and functional architecture before the invention of plywood. The reminder humbles—and strengthens—us."[11]

An awareness of the issues surrounding the modern building style was given a boost in America by the popularity of Ayn Rand's novel *The Fountainhead*, first published in 1943. While architecture itself was only incidental to Rand's philosophy of individualism, she glorified it—and abetted the imperiousness that came to be associated with its practitioners—by portraying her arrogant, self-reliant hero, Howard Roark, as an architect. She depicted for the readers of the four hundred thousand copies sold by 1948[12] a vision of what the architectural future might hold as they turned from the reliance on foreign achievement to their own resources: "The single shafts stood immeasurably tall, out of scale to the rest of the earth. They were of their own world, and they held up to the sky the statement of what man had conceived and made possible. They were empty molds. But man had come so far; he could go farther. The city on the edge of the sky held a question—and a promise."[13] The promise that would fill these empty molds would be functionalist architecture of a determinist, doctrinaire sort, didactically explained so that even the least sophisticated reader would understand it:

> "A house can have integrity, just like a person," said Roark, "and just as seldom."
> "In what way?"
> "Well, look at it. Every piece of it is there because the house needs it—and for no other reason. You see it from here as it is inside. The rooms in which you'll live made the shape. The relation of masses was determined by the distribution of space within. The ornament was determined by the method of construction, an emphasis of the principle that makes it stand. You can see each stress, each support that meets it. Your own eyes go through a structural process when you look at the house, you can follow each step, you see it rise, you know what made it and why it stands."[14]

The buildings that represented Roark's architecture for the 1949 film that Rand adapted from the novel were unfortunately mere pastiches of modernist designs (fig. 88). The thought of any such style taking over must have appalled the critic of *The New Yorker*, who reported that the "hero designs buildings so free from classical taint that they resemble waffle irons or upended tombstones."[15]

Buildings that shared the functionalist aesthetic were beginning to be constructed in America, principally by the émigrés from Nazi Germany who had conceived and developed it during the 1920s and were now transforming the International Style of architecture for the New World. In 1948 Walter Gropius and his firm The Architects Collaborative built the Harkness Commons dormitories at Harvard University (where he headed the Graduate School of Design), a startling invasion of modernism into a setting rife with tradition. Mies van der Rohe, who had begun to redesign the campus of the Illinois Institute of Technology (where he taught) in 1940, went on to complete a spectacular series of taut and elegant glass and steel structures, among them the 860–880 Lake Shore Drive apartment towers (1950–52) and Crown Hall at the Illinois Institute (1956) in Chicago, and the Seagram building on New York's Park Avenue (1957), which he designed with Philip Johnson, who had become his associate after having returned to Harvard to study architecture under Gropius. Their students (along with such firms as Skidmore, Owings and Merrill, designers of Lever House [fig. 89] in New York, which had been

88 Gary Cooper as Howard Roark (right) in a scene from *The Fountainhead*, 1949, adapted by Ayn Rand from her novel.

among the few progressives in American architecture in the 1930s), spread the International Style philosophy in ever-widening waves.

As such buildings were being constructed, their architects sought to furnish them in an appropriate style. Beginning in the late 1930s, the Museum of Modern Art had taken an active role in influencing the direction of contemporary design by exhibiting useful objects whose forms fit museum standards and by sponsoring competitions for new work in such areas as "organic design," low-cost furnishings, and lighting. Its visibility in this area expanded greatly with the series of "Good Design" exhibitions it organized annually between 1950 and 1955 in collaboration with the Merchandise Mart in Chicago. The exhibits were diverse in their styles, however, and directed toward the furnishing of domestic or modest interiors more than the grandiose institutional and corporate settings on which these architects were then setting their sights. There was a small pool of suitable designs by other emigrants from

Germany, such as Walter von Nessen, who had founded his own lighting concern in 1927 and whose widow Greta continued to create new works in an updated functionalist style (colorplate 17), but there was nothing that could satisfy the scale and the variety of needs of the new corporate endeavors, especially the luxurious and highly controlled buildings of Mies van der Rohe.

To begin to fill this gap, Hans Knoll Associates arranged in 1948 to bring Mies's "Barcelona" chair and several of his other pieces back into production. Knoll's firm was not then the international giant it is today, but a young company struggling to make an impact with modern furniture in America. Founded in 1938 by Hans Knoll (whose father, a manufacturer of progressive furniture in Germany, had had connections with Mies, Gropius, and Breuer), the firm was then beginning to replace its Danish-style wooden furniture

89 SKIDMORE, OWINGS AND MERRILL Lever House, New York, 1951.

with pieces designed in a functionalist style. Florence Schust Knoll, who had studied with Mies at the Armour Institute (later the Illinois Institute of Technology) in Chicago before going to work for Knoll (and marrying the boss), was the principal contact in bringing the "Barcelona" chair to Knoll. She herself worked in a derivative functionalist style created out of immediate need, providing Knoll with sofas and tables to be used en suite with the "Barcelona" group in the corporate interiors she was designing as part of Knoll's corporate design unit (colorplate 15).

Readying the "Barcelona" chair for production was not easy. The working drawings that had been made for the original production model were then in East Germany, along with most of Mies's early drawings, and Knoll had to reconstruct them from existing models.[16] Acting as a go-between, Philip Johnson, then taking a second term at the helm of the architecture and design department at the Museum of Modern Art, wrote to Mies in November 1947 "about [Knoll's] model of the Barcelona chair. They have finally manufactured it in steel with chromium plate, after unsuccessful attempts with aluminum. I believe it looks very well. There is only one dissappointment [*sic*], and that is that the steel is 1/32 of an inch thinner than the European. It adds to the springiness of the chair, but in my opinion not very much. They have made the leather cushions without buttons, which I also believe is satisfactory. They have promised not to make the chair in muslin, but only in material which is approved by you."[17]

Mies's immediate reaction seems to have been the handwritten notation in the margin of Johnson's letter asking "no contract?" Because Mies's furniture was not protected by patents, it could be manufactured and sold by anyone as long as his name was not used to promote it. As a savvy businessman Mies would have wanted to come quickly to an agreement with the manufacturer so he could be assured that his furniture would be made according to his standards and that it would be available for him to use in his own buildings. Moreover, this would allow him to stake out the market in what seemed like a proprietary fashion to discourage others from entering it. It may not have been until 1956, however, that Mies signed an encompassing agreement with Knoll, when he gave the company exclusive rights to manufacture and sell the "Barcelona" chair (and two other pieces) in the United States, Canada, France, Germany, and Belgium, receiving in turn five percent royalties and the assurance that he would be able to approve all models and samples and would be fully credited for the design in all publicity. He also reserved the right to manufacture the furniture himself, but only for his own use.[18]

Mies's second reaction to Johnson's letter was technical: he objected to the proposal for leather cushions without the buttons used in the prewar models.[19] Details of production continued to involve Johnson, who reported sev-

90 LUDWIG MIES VAN DER ROHE "Barcelona" chair, 1929. Made by Knoll Associates by 1953 (when it entered the museum). Chrome-plated steel and brown leather. Height 29½" (75 cm). The Museum of Modern Art, New York. Gift of the manufacturer. From Arthur Drexler and Greta Daniel, *Introduction to Twentieth Century Design from the Collection of the Museum of Modern Art, New York* (Garden City, N.Y., 1959). See also figs. 100 and 114.

eral months later, in February 1948: "I have just seen Hans Knoll's sample Barcelona Chair. The cushions that they have made are slightly thinner and more flexible than the original ones, and they are finished in cow-hide and welted much more coursely [*sic*] than your German ones. The frame of the chair is made of very slightly thinner strap steel than yours. This slight change, however, does not seem essential to me. The bad joints and poor welding job of the earlier models have been corrected, and in my opinion you could safely authorize their manufacture."[20]

With Mies's approval, Knoll issued the chair along with an ottoman and a table (originally a design for Tugendhat) that same year. The chair's chrome-plated frame of flat steel bars had become thinner and more refined (fig. 90),with the weld at the crossing considerably reduced from that of the prewar model (colorplate 13). Its construction changed with technology: the frame of the prewar model had been additive, made of two side sections joined to the cross pieces with bolts, while the Knoll model was constructed as a single unit, precisely cut and welded; in 1964, the chrome-plated construction was augmented by versions in stainless steel.[21] The upholstery also was altered in the various editions. The loose tufting forming a diagonal pattern seen in photographs of the Barcelona pavilion (fig. 75) became more tailored, and the buttons were welted in a regular grid pattern; with the introduction of foam in Knoll's 1964 model the cushions were made thicker and could maintain their more severe profile (fig. 100).

The "Barcelona" series was the only historical functionalist furniture that was marketed on a large scale for about a decade, and many of the significant buildings of the 1950s and early 1960s featured it, especially in their lobbies and executive suites. If architects wanted upscale, stylistically compatible furniture for their new glass and steel buildings, it was their first choice. For comparable workaday interiors, there were many other possibilities, anonymous corporate stuff distantly allied to those functionalist forms, manufactured and distributed by a large number of companies which were then outfitting the offspring of the postwar building boom. By early 1964, when Knoll had added four more Mies designs to its list, including the "Tugendhat" and "Brno" chairs (the latter were then revived for the Four Seasons restaurant, designed by Johnson, in the Seagram building), and published a small catalogue entitled *A Collection of Furniture by Mies van der Rohe*, their market had grown to be very lucrative.[22]

Faced with the success of Mies's furniture, other companies did not sit still; they began to knock it off. "Barcelona"-style chairs, stools, and tables, and "Brno"-style chairs were manufactured in stainless steel by Gratz Industries in New York, maker of "Fine Metal Fabrications."[23] Colonial Iron Craftsmen, also in New York, produced an awkward, debased version of the

"Barcelona" chair called the "Avanti" chair, with an enlarged vertical joining at the crossing of the legs—which it advertised in *Interior Design* magazine during most of 1964 (fig. 91)— along with an ottoman and a table with a glass top sitting on curving X-shaped supports. They offered the chair in two widths and as a settee, with a mirror or satin finish and the choice of "premiere Naugahyde," leather, or fabric upholstery.[24] Because of these competitively priced versions, Knoll was irate over an article that appeared in *Interiors* that same year describing the work of Gerry Griffith, "master craftsman in stainless steel."[25] It not only publicized the fact that Mies's designs were not under copyright but also mistakenly claimed that Griffith had been the first to bring Mies's furniture to market after the war. For years Mies had wanted to see his furniture produced in stainless steel, but until he arranged with Griffith to take up the task during the mid-1950s he had been unsuccessful in finding someone who could master the difficulties of working in this material, or in convincing Knoll to do it (they introduced stainless for

91 Advertisement for Colonial Iron Craftsmen's "Avanti" chair. From *Interior Design* (March 1964). The New York Public Library.

92 Gerry Griffith working on his stainless steel version of Ludwig Mies van der Rohe's "Barcelona" chair. From *Interiors* (November 1964). The New York Public Library.

some of his furniture only in 1964). "The main problem with stainless," Griffith explained, "is to bend it, and bring it to a mirror finish, which is what Mies wanted in the Barcelona chair."[26] The illustration of Griffith at work shows him with an extremely attenuated frame, sleek and seamless (fig. 92), considerably removed from the 1929 version and from Knoll's as well. Griffith's second triumph, the article announced, was his fabrication of the "Tugendhat" chair. After ten years of trying, he had created an alloy (which he copyrighted) that gave the "necessary resiliency" required to reproduce the chair "in true spring stainless."[27] These versions suggested the much more refined aesthetic that Mies was now able to demand, using alloys and techniques newly available. Whereas he had been comfortable enough to use colored models of the tubular-steel cantilever chairs made by Thonet in his own buildings, exhibitions, and interiors in the 1930s, and to allow manufacturers to sell his work with colored lacquer finishes (colorplate 5), when Knoll later suggested that the "Barcelona" range might be offered in a bronze finish, he was "absolutely against" the idea.[28] Bamberg had also used fabric along with leather upholstery, but Knoll originally upholstered theirs in only black or tan leather.

It did not take long for the Bauhaus Style to create its look. Mies led the way, aided by Philip Johnson, and others soon followed. Although in the prewar years Mies's interiors were sumptuous and richly colored, the postwar aesthetic left them cool and restrained. When Johnson created the decor for the Four Seasons restaurant in the Seagram building in 1959, his work was cited for its "exquisite refinement," which meant an almost monochromatic luxuriousness. "One singular paradox" of the four and one-half million dollar space, reported *Interiors*, "is that despite the exceptional richness of its materials and workmanship, it is essentially colorless and unobtrusive."[29] The interior was an amalgam of neutrals and metallics—natural and black leather, French walnut, travertine, and bronze, brass, gold, and silver, an elegant but safe neutrality that could only add to the self-importance of the corporate decision makers who congregated there. The lack of color in such spaces was so extreme that in describing the decor of the Seagram offices, which Johnson also had a hand in, *Interiors* pointed out that "the dress of the human occupants" offered "almost the only color throughout this neutral-hued, smoothly luminous, prodigally spacious domain."[30] A similar taste for neutrality was being applied to corporate offices by Florence Knoll, who revolutionized them in the 1950s, according to the *New York Times*: "Once upon a time virtually every big business executive thought—or whoever did his thinking for him on such matters thought—that his office had to have pale green walls and that his heavy, drawers-to-the-floor desk had to be placed cater-cornered. Then along came a woman who showed the executives that they could be just as impressive against a background of neutral or even white walls, sometimes with one wall in a strong primary color, and that their status would not be impaired if they moved their desks into a logical, space-saving four-square position."[31] This was written at the time Knoll was designing the interiors for the CBS building in New York, which were four square, in rigid and angular arrangements, and neutral in tone except for the occasional color accent (colorplate 15).

The prominent success of the Bauhaus Style at such high levels of spending in America spurred interest in Europe in reviving the metal furniture of Marcel Breuer and Le Corbusier, Jeanneret, and Perriand. In the immediate postwar period, the Thonet firm in East Germany, where its factories had been bombed and materials were restricted, was in no position to resume large-scale manufacturing, especially in metal, and did not reintroduce its tubular-metal lines until 1957; the independent American Thonet company saw no market for them at that time either, and did not bring them back until 1959.[32] In 1949, still smarting under the terms of their 1920s contract with Thonet, Le Corbusier had written his cousin Pierre Jeanneret: "I intend to try to put back on track the two armchairs and the chaise longue from 1929 that Ch. Perriand and the two of us collaborated on."[33] Frustration turned into outrage, however, when in 1952 "a rich Brazilian" told him that she had bought a chaise longue from a store that sold modern furniture in Zurich: "There, they are making this chaise longue and I know nothing about it! And I have never seen a penny from the royalties. I find that unbelievable!" he wrote to Willy Boesiger, the Swiss architect and editor of a catalogue of his buildings, describing his plight and enlisting Boesiger's aid. "I would like to have a chaise longue for my wife, who needs to rest with her legs elevated," he continued somewhat pathetically. "Could I ask you to make inquiries and protest strenuously on my behalf demanding that they pay the royalties and send me a chaise longue here as compensation."[34] The answer he received from Wohnbedarf, the department store in Zurich known since the 1930s for its progressive interior design, gave him a realistic assessment of the interest in functionalism in Europe during the early 1950s and of how the control of his works had deteriorated:

> We generally pay license fees for models that are registered, which in our opinion, is not the case for yours, at least not in Switzerland.... Before the war, your model was found in the Thonet catalogue. For Switzerland, Thonet had given the manufacturing license to the Swiss corporation Fabricants de Meubles en Fer, a corporation composed of
> Embru S.A., Rueti/Zch
> Bigla S.A., Biglen/Be
> Fabrique Bâloise de Meubles en Fer S.A., Sissach (Bâle).
> An illustration of your chaise longue is found in the catalogues of these firms. We ourselves bought it from these firms. We do not know if Thonet on their part paid you license fees with regard to the undertaking in question. After the war, this furniture was not being made anywhere—thus we took it upon ourselves to have the few isolated pieces that we need made by our house metalworker, without any question of having to get our own license.[35]

Le Corbusier began to consider alternatives, one of his thoughts being to enter into a contract with Herman Miller, the American furniture company that had hired George Nelson as its advisor and started manufacturing the designs of Charles Eames, but at this time, about 1953, he still considered himself contractually bound to Thonet.[36] Finally, at the end of the decade, he took a stand: acknowledging that examples of the furniture were being produced by Wohnbedarf and others and claiming he had received virtually no royalties from Thonet in thirty years, he decided to disregard the firm's claims and arranged to license the furniture again.[37] New drawings were made under the supervision of Charlotte Perriand,[38] fabrication was overseen by Willy Boesiger, and a small edition of four designs—the chair with adjustable back, two sizes of the "Grand Confort" armchair, and the chaise longue—was issued for an exhibition in 1959 at the gallery of Heidi Weber in Zurich. The tubular-steel frames were made in nickel or chrome plate, the chaise and the adjustable armchair were both offered in pony skin or fabric, and the loose horsehair and down cushions of the "Grand Confort" models were covered in leather or fabric.[39] The three designers shared in the receipts when Le Corbusier signed a long-term contract with a French manufacturer to produce the furniture for Weber,[40] but the designs were sold solely under the name of Le Corbusier, much to Perriand's annoyance.[41] "Le Corbusier" alone was used to designate the line when in 1965 production was taken over and expanded by the Italian furniture manufacturer Cassina (and it still is today).[42] Cassina's versions were produced in nickel-plated or enameled tubular steel with leather or pony-skin upholstery, and the "Grand Confort" models were now cushioned in foam, which gave them firmer seats and more severely geometric forms. Adding to their status and helping to justify the high price tag that resulted from the many hours of hand fabrication and the expensive upholstery materials, the furniture was now engraved with Le Corbusier's signature and numbered—"a distinction not accorded Corbusier seating designs produced by other manufacturers," the *New York Times* reported, adding, without additional comment, "possibly because all these designs were done originally in collaboration with two other people."[43]

Marcel Breuer's designs were also revived at this time in Italy by Dino Gavina at the furniture company that bears his name. Gavina was partial to designs such as Breuer's that had been conceived for industrial manufacture. Earlier he had rejected an offer to collaborate with Heidi Weber on reissuing the Le Corbusier-Jeanneret-Perriand furniture because "Breuer's product was designed for mass production; Le Corbusier's was not. Le Corbusier's furniture, if mass produced, would have been flunked at any average school for industrial design," he explained. "If... we examine the famous cube ["Grand Confort"] armchair by Le Corbusier, what do we notice? The tube is used with six corner welds, plus two head welds, and six more welds that join the (hollow) tube to the (solid) reinforcing bar, and we can add to these the four corner welds that join the L-iron to the frame, and we have a total of eighteen manual welding operations for a single piece of furniture, to which we must add the use of inconsistent materials: three different materials welded one to another in the same structure, which is sheer madness, in terms of industrial manufacture."[44] Gavina reissued only three examples from among Breuer's many metal furniture designs. Now they were given names for merchandising purposes: "Wassily" for the club chair, after the painter Wassily Kandinsky, who had admired it and encouraged Breuer to keep working on his metal furniture; "Cesca" for the caned side chair, after Gavina's daughter Francesca; and "Laccio" for the small table, an Italianiza-

93 KAJ FRANCK
Pitchers, designed 1954, for Nuutajärvi Glass. Clear and colored glass. Height 8 5/8" (22 cm). Iittala Glass, Iittala, Finland.

tion of Breuer's middle name, Lajko.[45] Thonet, when it began to manufacture Breuer's work again, had pretty much followed the original designs, but Breuer made subtle adjustments when Gavina contracted for new models in 1962 and continued to revise them after Knoll acquired Gavina,[46] with the overall appearance becoming smoother and more elegant. Closer tolerances were used for the joints, and the bolts, which were very apparent in the original models (fig. 59) although they had been airbrushed out in the Thonet catalogues (frontispiece), were minimized.

By the mid-1960s the revival of functionalist furniture was in full swing—"*de rigueur* for avant-garde interiors," wrote the *New York Times*. "These pieces," the article continued, "are not considered antiques but creations that have caught the modern spirit."[47] This modern spirit also supported a reinterpretation of the type of industrially inspired tablewares that had been issued in the 1930s, among them Kaj Franck's elegant adaptation of laboratory forms in 1954 for the Finnish manufacturer Nuutajärvi (fig. 93), and spurred a serious, if limited, expression of neofunctionalism in furniture beginning in the mid-1950s. Some designers updated 1920s forms in a very sophisticated manner, such as the German Helmut Magg, whose caned tubular-steel side chair (fig. 94) echoes Mies's cantilever version (colorplate 5), while others looked to the same sources as had the earlier designers. A 1961 folding metal and canvas stool in a traditional form by the Dane Poul Kjaerholm paralleled Le Corbusier's adaptation of the traveling chair in the 1920s and similar borrowings by his compatriots Kaare Klint and Mogens Koch in the 1930s.[48] Most of Kjaerholm's mature furniture production, beginning in the mid-1950s, was a fantasy on functionalism; he was one of the only Europeans to work continuously in this revival style, creating serviceable tables, chairs, desks, and sofas of metal, glass, leather, and cane for upscale office furnishing, as well as revitalized forms that tested the limits of functionalist premises (fig. 95).[49] In the United States, George Nelson created the paradigmatic neofunctionalist work in 1964, a tubular-steel and leather sofa that was touted as the first couch inducted into the collection of the Museum of Modern Art (colorplate 16).

94 HELMUT MAGG
Chair, c. 1960. Steel and rattan. Height 31" (79 cm). Private collection, Munich.

95 POUL KJAERHOLM
"Hammock" chair, 1965.
Made by E. Kold Christensen, Copenhagen. Steel and cane. Length 61″ (155 cm). Danske Kunstindustrimuseum, Copenhagen.

Not only did it adopt much of the stylistic vocabulary of the 1920s, achieving a virtual seamlessness that suggested fabrication from a single piece of tubular metal, but it also was created fully in a new spirit of functionalism. In working out his design, Nelson was concerned equally with the comfort of the sofa and the integration of modern materials and production methods new to furniture making, such as the use of epoxy to achieve the precision of its joints.

The renewed functionalist style was brought into domestic interiors as highly paid architects began to build and furnish houses for their corporate clients, transferring the same austere formality from office to home. In the United States, this could hardly have happened otherwise, since reeditions and revivalist pieces were sold in off-limits showrooms, available only to designers, architects, decorators, and their clients. The core of the design scheme was simply the rigid arrangement of the Barcelona pavilion and Mies van der Rohe's houses (figs. 75–77; 97) in a formula that was to be copied time and again in office buildings and in homes (and illustrated in magazines and

96 TOIVO KORHONEN
Living room of the architect's house, Lauttasaari, near Helsinki.

97 LUDWIG MIES VAN DER ROHE
860–880 Lake Shore Drive Apartments, Chicago. A northeast corner living room, interior perspective, c. 1951. Ink, pencil, watercolor, and silver print on illustration board. The Museum of Modern Art, New York, Mies van der Rohe Archive. Gift of the architect.

books) during the 1960s in the United States and on distant shores (fig. 96). Even when the furnishings strayed totally from the Bauhaus Style, the formulaic rigidity of their placement remained (fig. 98). Limited access kept the revival at an elite level, made the classic works into status symbols, and confirmed the aura that made them seem like museum pieces.

And of course they were. For years reeditions were the principal way in which fans could confront European functionalist design, and these models began to be seen on platforms in museums. The Museum of Modern Art, the only art institution with a curatorial department dedicated to collecting design, began to exhibit works from its permanent collection extensively in 1958, when a major exhibition was held (fig. 99), and permanently in 1964, when the museum unveiled its first design galleries. Even when earlier models were in the museum's collection or available for acquisition, the sleeker reeditions were often preferred to the originals, and always upholstered in neutral Bauhaus Style tones. A Knoll version of the "Barcelona" chair, for example, has always been its model of choice for exhibition in the design galleries. This chair was acquired in 1953 fitted with the thin cushions (in tan leather) mentioned in Philip Johnson's letter to Mies van der Rohe (fig. 90). Disregarding the integrity of the design object, the Museum of Modern Art

98 HARRY SEIDLER AND ASSOCIATES
Living room of house at Pymble, New South Wales, Australia.

99 "20th-Century Design from the Museum Collection," The Museum of Modern Art, New York, 1958–59.

in 1964 replaced the original cushions with thicker ones, in tan leather (fig. 100), from the redesigned Knoll production, and then in 1985 reupholstered them in white kid leather as an allusion to the original upholstery in the Barcelona pavilion (fig. 114).[50] None of this is explained in the gallery and what the visitor sees is a complete hybrid: a German chair seemingly from 1929 made in America before 1953 with its cushions redesigned in 1964 and reupholstered in 1985. It is impossible to pinpoint the chair as it is today to a specific moment in the history of design, and it stands, instead, as a summation of the conflations inherent in the Bauhaus Style.

"Bauhaus" was the rubric used by the Museum of Modern Art to bring functionalist design together, a term acknowledged in its 1959 *Introduction to Twentieth Century Design* to be "still popularly (if often incorrectly) used to describe whatever seems 'functional' or 'modern.'" Its popularity (and its inaccuracy) was encouraged by the museum through its repetitive focus on the school, which it called "the focal point in the integration of design with the machine age."[51] This had commercial repercussions, such as the revivalist "New Bauhaus" chair in the Stendig catalogue (fig. 86) and an advertisement by the same company for the famous nineteenth-century Thonet bentwood armchair used by Le Corbusier, which it labeled "Pre-Bauhaus."[52] The use of this generic label was also encouraged by an ecumenicalism among scholars—for example, Hans M. Wingler, whose mammoth study of the Bauhaus, first published in Germany in 1962,[53] devoted six full pages to the work of Mies van der Rohe from the decade before he ever became associated with the school (his work was given a similar treatment by the museum's *Introduction*, which also included Le Corbusier under the Bauhaus heading[54])—as if influence only radiated from the Bauhaus, thereby denying the independence and early importance of Mies and his Berlin group of architects and the work of Le Corbusier. What made each of the original functionalist endeavors distinct conceptually, historically, and stylistically—Breuer's concern for production, Mies's mania for materials and luxuriousness, Le Corbusier's focus on types and the undeniable stylishness of his firm's work—came to be overlooked in this way under the influence of those who zeroed in on what made reeditions of their works superficially alike—the absolute congruity of materials, their cool sense of austerity, and the monochromatic palette imposed under the influence of Machine Art by important architects, corporate manufacturers, and their well-trained clientele.

100 The Museum of Modern Art's example of Ludwig Mies van der Rohe's "Barcelona" chair made by Knoll Associates by 1953 (fig. 90) after being reupholstered in 1964 in tan leather with thicker cushions. The seat no longer has a trapezoidal profile and the frame is said to be of stainless steel. From Ludwig Glaeser, *Ludwig Mies van der Rohe: Furniture and Furniture Drawings from the Design Collection and the Mies van der Rohe Archive* (New York, 1977).

Notes

1 Walter Dexel, "The Bauhaus Style – A Myth" [1964], in Eckhard Neumann, ed., *Bauhaus and Bauhaus People* (New York: Van Nostrand Reinhold Company, 1970), p. 107.

2 A summation of which Bill published in 1952 in his *Form: A Balance Sheet of Mid-Twentieth-Century Trends in Design* (Basel: K. Werner, 1952).

3 See Kathryn B. Hiesinger and George H. Marcus, *Landmarks of Twentieth-Century Design* (New York: Abbeville Press, 1993), pp. 147–213.

4 Kay Fisker, "The Moral of Functionalism," *Magazine of Art* 43 (February 1950), p. 66.

5 Philip C. Johnson, *Ludwig Mies van der Rohe* (New York: The Museum of Modern Art, 1947).

6 Giulio Carlo Argan, *Walter Gropius e la Bauhaus* (Turin: Giulio Einaudi Editore, 1951).

7 Walter Gropius, quoted in Akio Izutsu, *The Bauhaus: A Japanese Perspective and a Profile of Hans and Florence Schust Knoll* (Tokyo: Kajima Institute Publishing Company, 1992), p. 52.

8 Edward Robert De Zurko, *Origins of Functionalist Theory* (New York: Columbia University Press, 1957), p. 239.

9 Horatio Greenough, *Form and Function: Remarks on Art, Design, and Architecture*, edited by Harold A. Small, reprint (Berkeley and Los Angeles: University of California Press, 1958). These essays were taken from Henry T. Tuckerman's *Memorial of Horatio Greenough* (New York: G. P. Putnam, 1853).

10 Erle Loran, Introduction, in Greenough, *Form and Function*, pp. XIII–XXI.

11 Joseph Hudnut [review], *Magazine of Art* 41 (March 1948), p. 114.

12 See Barbara Branden, *The Passion of Ayn Rand* (Garden City, N. Y.: Doubleday and Company, 1986), pp. 175–81.

13 Ayn Rand, *The Fountainhead* [1943] (New York: The New American Library, 1964), p. 192.

14 Ibid., p. 128.

15 John McCarten, The Current Cinema: "Down with Beaux Arts," *The New Yorker*, July 16, 1949, p. 46.

16 The drawings had been with the architect Edward Ludwig in Berlin, and were not returned until 1964 (Dr. Ludwig Glaeser to Gene Summers [Mies office], August 10, 1965, Mies van der Rohe Archives, Library of Congress, Washington, D. C., Museum of Modern Art 1963–69 folder). Similarly, when Knoll was working to reissue the "Tugendhat" chair in 1963, Mies's office told Knoll to follow the specifications of the chair at the Museum of Modern Art (Gene R. Summers to Vincent Cafiero [Knoll office], November 4, 1963, in ibid). The following correspondence is from the Library of Congress's Mies van der Rohe Archives.

17 Philip C. Johnson to Ludwig Mies van der Rohe, November 26, 1947, in ibid., Museum of Modern Art 1940–47 folder.

18 Mies van der Rohe and Knoll Associates, Agreement, November 8, 1956, in ibid., Knoll Associates 1956–64 folder.

19 Felix C. Bonnet [Mies office] to Philip C. Johnson, December 1, 1947, in ibid., Museum of Modern Art 1940–47 folder.

20 Philip C. Johnson to Ludwig Mies van der Rohe, February 27, 1948, in ibid., Museum of Modern Art 1948–50 folder.

21 Undated Knoll specification list [c. 1964], in ibid., Knoll Associates 1956–64 folder.

22 In one three-month period, Knoll sold 101 "Barcelona" chairs, 22 stools, 113 tables, and 92 "Brno" chairs, with an income of close to $90,000 and royalties for Mies of $4,461; royalty statement, December 1964–February 1965, in ibid., Knoll Associates 1965–74 folder.

23 Undated tear sheet, in ibid., Furniture folder.

24 Robert Garvin Associates, Inc. [sales agent], press release and price list, dated March and July 1964, in ibid.

25 "Gerry Griffith: Master Craftsman in Stainless Steel," *Interiors* 124 (November 1964), pp. 74, 75, 144, 146.

26 Ibid., p. 144.

27 Ibid., p. 75.

28 Peter Carter [Mies office] to Vincent Cafiero, August 9, 1967, Mies van der Rohe Archives, Library of Congress, Washington, D. C., Knoll Associates 1965–74 folder.

29 "The Four Seasons," *Interiors* 119 (December 1959), pp. 80, 82.

30 John Anderson, "Seagram Building: Interiors in Keeping with a Masterpiece," *Interiors* 118 (December 1958), p. 76.

31 Virginia Lee Warren, "The Woman Who Led Office Revolution Rules an Empire of

Modern Design," *New York Times*, September 1, 1964, p. C40.

32 See Christopher Wilk, *Thonet: 150 Years of Furniture* (Woodbury, N. Y., and London: Barron's, 1980), pp. 121, 122, 131.

33 Le Corbusier to Pierre Jeanneret, March 31, 1949, Le Corbusier Archives, Fondation Le Corbusier, Paris, F1 (3) Meubles, doc. 189.

34 Le Corbusier to Willy Boesiger, July 7, 1952, in ibid., doc. 196.

35 Wohnbedarf, Zurich, to Le Corbusier, September 10, 1952, in ibid., doc. 197.

36 Le Corbusier to MM Chereau, Wogensky, and Ducret, "Information au sujet de l'affaire 'Chaise-longue Thonet'" [undated, c. 1953], in ibid., doc. 273.

37 Le Corbusier, "Note à l'attention de Monsieur A. P. Ducret" [business manager], January 8, 1959, in ibid., doc. 245.

38 Copies of the drawings for the chaise longue and the chair with adjustable back are in ibid., docs. 232–41.

39 Heidi Weber [gallery], Zurich, *Le Corbusier 1929: Sièges, Sitzmöbel, Chairs* (November 1959), catalogue leaflet, Fondation Le Corbusier, Paris, pamphlet files.

40 A. P. Ducret to Charlotte Perriand, March 23, 1960, Le Corbusier Archives, Fondation Le Corbusier, Paris, F1 (3) Meubles, doc. 247.

41 Charlotte Perriand to Polytech, Paris, June 23, 1966, in ibid., doc. 258.

42 Franco Cassina, quoted in Rita Reif, "Young Men Hope to Sell Le Corbusier Furniture in Volume," *New York Times*, March 14, 1967, p. 50.

43 Ibid.

44 Dino Gavina, *Casa Vogue*, no. 78 (January 1978); translated in Virgilio Vercelloni, *The Adventure of Design: Gavina* (New York: Rizzoli, 1989), p. 14.

45 Eric Larrabee and Massimo Vignelli, *Knoll Design* (New York: Harry N. Abrams Publishers, 1981), p. 172.

46 See Elaine Louie, "The Many Lives of a Very Common Chair," *New York Times*, February 7, 1991, p. C10.

47 Barbara Plumb, "They Coined 'Modern' More Than 30 Years Ago," *New York Times Magazine*, April 3, 1966, p. 78.

48 See David Revere McFadden, ed., *Scandinavian Modern Design, 1880–1980* (New York: Harry N. Abrams Publishers, 1982), pp. 205, 120, 123.

49 See Per Mollerup, "Poul Kjaerholm's Furniture," *Mobilia*, no. 304–5 (1982), pp. 1–24.

50 Matilda McQuaide, Assistant Curator, Department of Architecture and Design, The Museum of Modern Art, New York, to the author, July 29, 1994.

51 Arthur Drexler, Introduction, in Arthur Drexler and Greta Daniel, *Introduction to Twentieth Century Design from the Collection of the Museum of Modern Art, New York* (Garden City, N. Y.: Doubleday and Company, 1959), p. 34.

52 See *Interior Design* 35 (September 1964), p. 3.

53 Hans M. Wingler, *The Bauhaus: Weimar Dessau Berlin Chicago* (Cambridge, Mass., and London: The MIT Press, 1969).

54 See Drexler and Daniel, *Twentieth Century Design*, pp. 34–47. This continues today. An advertisement for Knoll in *The New York Times* "celebrating 75 years of Bauhaus design" depicted the "Barcelona" chair, made before Mies was associated with the school (November 10, 1994, p. C12).

Where Are We At?

Functionalism, Yes, But.

Robert Venturi and Denise Scott Brown[1]

By the late 1970s functionalism was a sinking ship. *The Titanic*, Stanley Tigerman's photomontage of Mies van der Rohe's modernist icon Crown Hall going under (fig. 101), can only be seen as emblematic of the state in which functionalism found itself late in the century. With the faceless monotony of the rebuilt city, the "cataclysmic purism of contemporary urban renewal," which, according to the architectural historian Vincent Scully, had "brought so many cities to the brink of catastrophe,"[2] and the conservatism and elitism of corporate patronage, very little was left of the ideals and ambitions that had launched it.

The rumblings had been felt much earlier, however, at first mainly in print, as architects, designers, and critics began to question the relevance of

101 STANLEY TIGERMAN
The Titanic, 1978. Photomontage. 11 x 14" (28 x 35.7 cm). The Art Institute of Chicago. Gift of Stanley Tigerman.

102 PHILIP JOHNSON
Model of American Telephone and Telegraph Building, New York, 1978.

the modernist aesthetic. In 1960 Philip Johnson, who had bound the Museum of Modern Art to the International Style and the Machine Art aesthetic, whose Glass House in New Canaan, Connecticut (1949–50),[3] had become a paradigm of the elegant absolutism of functionalist purity, and who had defined the syntax of the postwar functionalist interior, publicly gave it all up. A turncoat, he announced his "dislike" of the International Style in the *Architectural Review*; disdainful of existing "styles or disciplines," he asked "where are we at?" and wondered "can't we just wander around aimlessly?,"[4] which he himself seems to have done, using disparate historical sources and allusions as inspiration for the structures he then built.[5] His stylistic quest culminated almost two decades later in the American Telephone and Telegraph building in New York (fig. 102), a curiously postmodern appropriation

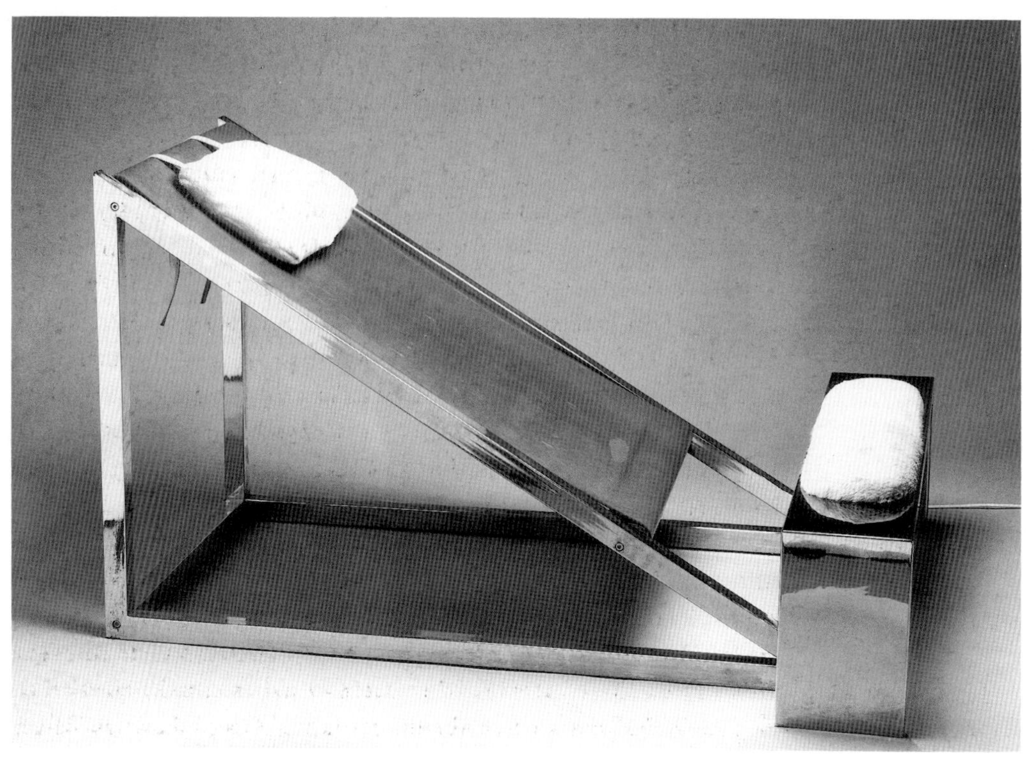

103 ARCHIZOOM ASSOCIATI
"Mies" chair and stool, 1969. Chrome-plated steel and rubber. Length 71 1/4" (181 cm). Museum für Kunst und Gewerbe, Hamburg.

that turned design—a Chippendale highboy suffering from gigantism— into architecture. Johnson's reversal came in a review of *Theory and Design in the First Machine Age*,[6] a collection of essays by Reyner Banham, editor of *Architectural Review*, who in this and other writings rejected the "common dependence on laws of form that were objective, absolute, universal and eternally valid" that followed from the ideas of Le Corbusier and Walter Gropius. "We live in a throw-away economy," he wrote, and "it is clearly absurd to demand that objects designed for a short useful life should exhibit qualities signifying eternal validity—such qualities as *divine* proportion, *pure* form or *harmony* of color."[7]

Robert Venturi, writing in 1966 in what he called his "Gentle Manifesto," *Complexity and Contradiction in Architecture*, denounced "the puritanically moral language of orthodox Modern architecture." Opening the way to a new style of modernism, he proclaimed: "I like elements which are hybrid rather than 'pure,' compromising rather than 'clean,' distorted rather than 'straightforward,' ambiguous rather than 'articulated,' perverse as well as impersonal, boring as well as 'interesting,' conventional rather than 'designed,' accommodating rather than excluding, redundant rather than simple, vestigial as well as innovating, inconsistent and equivocal rather than direct and clear. . . . I am for richness of meaning rather than clarity of meaning; for the implicit function as well as the explicit function."[8]

Designers took their own swipes on a polemical level at the concept of absolute and eternally valid forms. In Italy the radical design group Archizoom raised one of the very first challenges to functionalism on its own terms with their "Mies" chair, designed in 1969 (fig. 103). Signaling their target with the name of its then most-heralded designer, and adopting shiny metal (the material most closely associated with functionalism) and geometric form (following the letter if not the spirit of the dogma in their choice of a triangular shape), Archizoom conceived a chair that had a richness, rather than a clarity, of meaning. In the ambiguity of how this seemingly rigid and unyielding object was to be used—the slanted rubber seat gently gives under the weight of the sitter to form an armchair, and returns to its forbidding shape when the sitter rises—they questioned the concept that geometry is necessarily the basis of clear and logical design. A decade later, another Italian designer, Alessandro Mendini, discarded the obliqueness of Archizoom's reference and made a direct hit with a series of altered icons of modernism exhibited under the title "Redesign of Modern Movement Chairs." Among them was Marcel

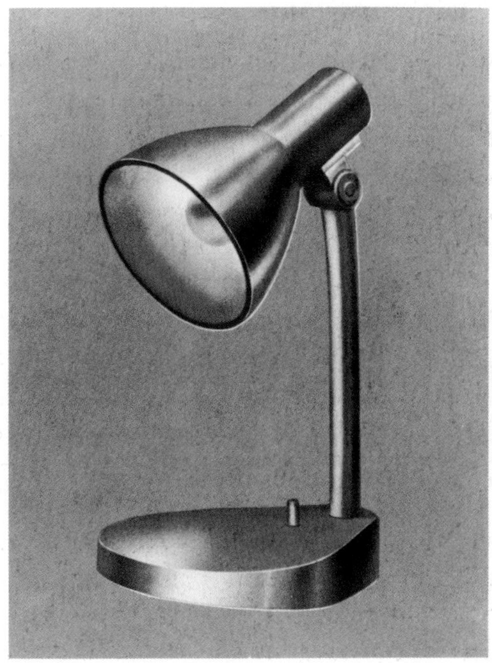

104 ALESSANDRO MENDINI
"Lamp without Light" (redesigned lamp by Marianne Brandt), 1975. Made by Bracciodiferro for Cassina. Bronze.

Breuer's "Wassily" chair, to which he had added painted decorations that interrupted and extended its rectilinear outline (colorplate 18). With these excrescences Mendini controverted Breuer's anonymous, mechanistic approach and announced a rival aesthetic of incongruity, irregularity, color, and ornamentation, raising high the standard of Italian postmodernism.

Mendini had already taken on Marianne Brandt's "Kandem" lamp (fig. 46), one of the great successes of the Bauhaus marriage of design and industry, with his own version in bronze for Cassina (fig. 104), which lacked accommodation for a light bulb. Like Jasper Johns's sculptures of beer cans and paintbrushes, Mendini's "lamp" added value to a common object by casting it in an artistic material. A work already ensconced in the pantheon of design was elevated further, removed from utility and transformed into an *objet d'art* to be appreciated for its form alone. In an analogous move, the American artist Scott Burton, who chose furniture as his sculptural medium, appropriated the standard, comfortable, Maple & Company armchair used by Le Corbusier in the Pavillon de l'Esprit Nouveau in 1925 (fig. 40) and memorialized it in granite, not removing it completely from utility but altering it from a soft fireside seat

105 SCOTT BURTON
Lounge chair, 1983. Granite. Estate of Scott Burton.

106 MARIO BOTTA
"Second" chair, 1982. Made by Alias. Painted steel and foam rubber. Height 28 3/8" (72 cm). Alias, Milan.

107 SCOTT BURTON
"Sling" chair, 1982–83. Tubular steel and leather. Private collection.

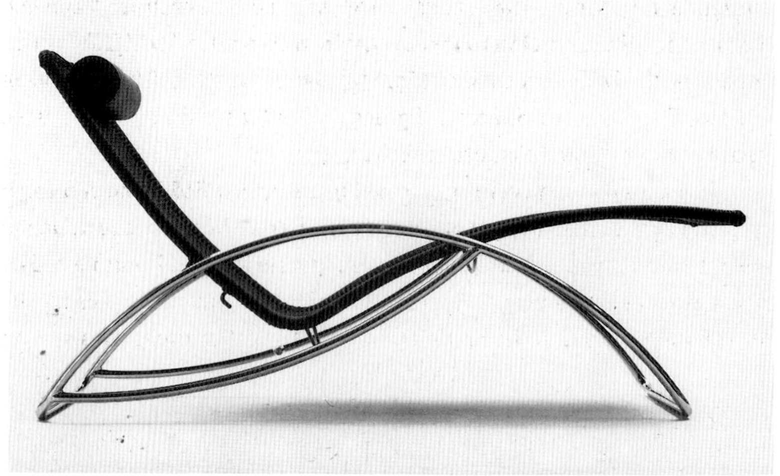

108 TORBEN SKOV
"Still Life" chaise longue, 1987. Made by Gebrüder Thonet GmbH, Frankenberg, Germany. Chrome-plated steel, synthetic upholstery, and leather. Length 70⅞" (180 cm). Die Neue Sammlung, Munich.

to a hard park bench (fig. 105).[9] As much as a decade later, when the battle against functionalism would already have seemed to be passé, the confrontations continued. In 1989 Coop Himmelblau, an architectural cooperative established in Vienna, deconstructed the most sumptuous of 1920s metal designs, the Le Corbusier-Jeanneret-Perriand "Grand Confort" armchair (colorplate 19), canting its cushions and seemingly unraveling its chrome skeleton and letting it trail on the floor (colorplate 20). By this time, however, in the face of what seemed an early exhaustion of stylistic postmodernism, this could also have been read as a statement of reconstruction, a wistful yearning for the quality and standards promoted by functionalism, suggested by the armchair's support, however precarious, on a solid architectural I-beam.

If these works mirrored a broad rejection of the dogmatism of what in the 1960s and 1970s was defined as functionalism, the specters of Breuer, Mies, and Le Corbusier had not lost their power to influence. Their materials, their forms, their conceits remained as inspirations into the 1980s—blatantly borrowed or subtly evoked—for a number of designers whose work for production focused on formalist solutions. The Swiss architect Mario Botta played with the geometry of Breuer's open cube in his "First" and "Second" chairs (fig. 106), melding it, in addition, with a requisite functionalist device, the cylindrical pillow. Scott Burton, now with a more faithful allegiance to his models in his choice of materials for his "Sling" chair—the only one he anticipated for actual production, having prepared a patent application for it—was formally ambivalent as he wavered between runners and legs and between an upright and a lounge form (fig. 107). Debts to the Le Corbusier-Jeanneret-Perriand furniture are clear in the adjustable, tubular-steel "Still Life" chaise longue by the Dane Torben Skov (fig. 108) and in the "Onda" (Wave) sofa of De Pas, D'Urbino, and Lomazzi (fig. 109), a fluid, curvilinear riposte to the angular, cubic "Grand Confort" armchair.

Such allusions and borrowings could be easily justified in the climate of refined historicism that had emerged as a factor in architecture and design in the 1970s, running parallel to a new ornamentalism tentatively introduced by Mendini's Studio Alchimia in Milan in 1976 and forcefully taken up by the Memphis group in its first collection in 1980. The excited reaction to

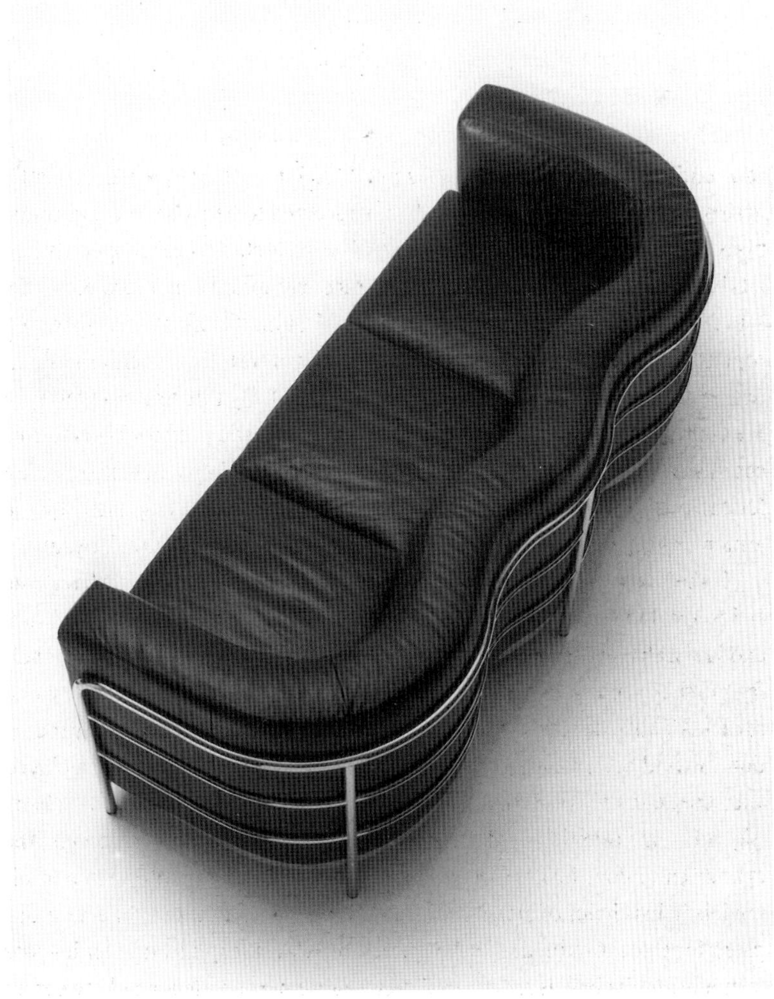

109 DE PAS, D'URBINO, AND LOMAZZI
"Onda" sofa, 1985. Made by Zanotta S.p.A. Stainless steel and leather. Length 76¾" (195 cm). Zanotta S.p.A., Nova Milanese, Italy.

their brash endeavors was unexpected, and manufacturers from Milan to America's furniture center, High Point, North Carolina, jumped on the bandwagon of the first fresh decorative style in half a century. This brought unexpected competition to the corporate design market as clients began to turn from the formulaic aesthetic and functionalist icons they had depended upon for years to more eccentric Milan-inspired designs complete with strong colors and bold patterns. In an attempt to save their share of the market, manufacturers of functionalist classics updated their own lines, with Cassina in 1980 introducing a new palette to their Le Corbusier furniture, principally earth tones drawn from the designer's own color schemes and selected with the help of Charlotte Perriand that were used for both upholstery and frames.[10] By the late 1980s the same collection was updated again and offered in an even larger variety of colors and combinations (colorplate 19). Color was finally also acknowledged by the Museum of Modern Art as an element of functionalist design when a number of works by Mies van der Rohe were shown upholstered in unexpected hues, including deep red and blue, in its 1977 retrospective of his furniture (colorplate 21). Yet the catalogue, with its metallic cover and exclusively black-and-white images, as well as the museum's permanent design galleries, continued to adhere to the Bauhaus Style preference for neutrality.[11]

The core works of Breuer, Mies, and Le Corbusier now fill a niche as one of the many historical styles that may be selected for interior decoration, totally removed from their independent aesthetic associations; they are regarded along with reissues of Charles Rennie Mackintosh's chairs, Jean-Michel Frank's sofas, Charles Eames's lounge chairs, and Isamu Noguchi's tables as the "classics of modern furniture" (fig. 110). Robert Venturi clearly

110 Advertisement for Palazzetti's "Classics of Modern Furniture." From *The New York Times* (May 20, 1993).

111 Functionalist icons in a Structure store.

acknowledged their new status at the Penn State Faculty Club in State College, Pennsylvania, in 1977, where he combined Mies's "Brno" chairs from Knoll, upholstered in a chevron-patterned cut velvet, with Chippendale reproductions, and *Progressive Architecture* affirmed his eclecticism by stating that "an informal mix of traditional (whether American vernacular or classic high-design modern) furniture has been used throughout."[12]

The exclusive elitism that wooed buyers in the 1960s and 1970s no longer works. In models described by manufacturers and retailers variously as editions, reproductions, and "authorized" versions, or dubbed "knockoffs" by critics, functionalist furniture can be had at a variety of price levels, within a wide range of quality of manufacture and choice of materials. Lacking patent and copyright protection, they now may come with the names of their designers and the original nomenclature of the models attached. These works are sold in shops and through catalogues, one of which offers them sandwiched between pages devoted to hand-carved Italian bombé chests,[13] a melange that would have been unthinkable two decades ago. They have also been co-opted as part of the lifestyle merchandising of fashion.[14] Structure, an apparel chain, evokes the image of the architect as a style-setter with its Palladian logo and its shops furnished with tubular-steel icons (fig. 111). Faced with the increased competition of cheaper versions of their own designs and of suddenly popular alternative styles, the leading American distributors, formerly satisfied with a restricted clientele in their showrooms, all at once became accessible in the late 1980s and 1990s. Knoll opened a store in New York's flashy Soho section and embarked on a catchy newspaper advertising campaign to market its classic furniture, while Atelier International, then distributor of Cassina's Le Corbusier line in the United States, responded by cutting prices.[15]

According to a survey of the market by the *New York Times*,[16] Marcel Breuer's popular caned "Cesca" chair could be bought in New York in 1991 at prices ranging from 45 to 813 dollars (the latter an authorized Gavina version from Knoll with Breuer's later alterations; fig. 112). While the cheaper chairs relied on less durable materials and revealed shortcuts in production, particularly in the bending of the steel tubes and in using machine-woven caning, their form was essentially the same, and for one of the copyists the

112 MARCEL BREUER
The Knoll Cesca Chair Collection, 1994.

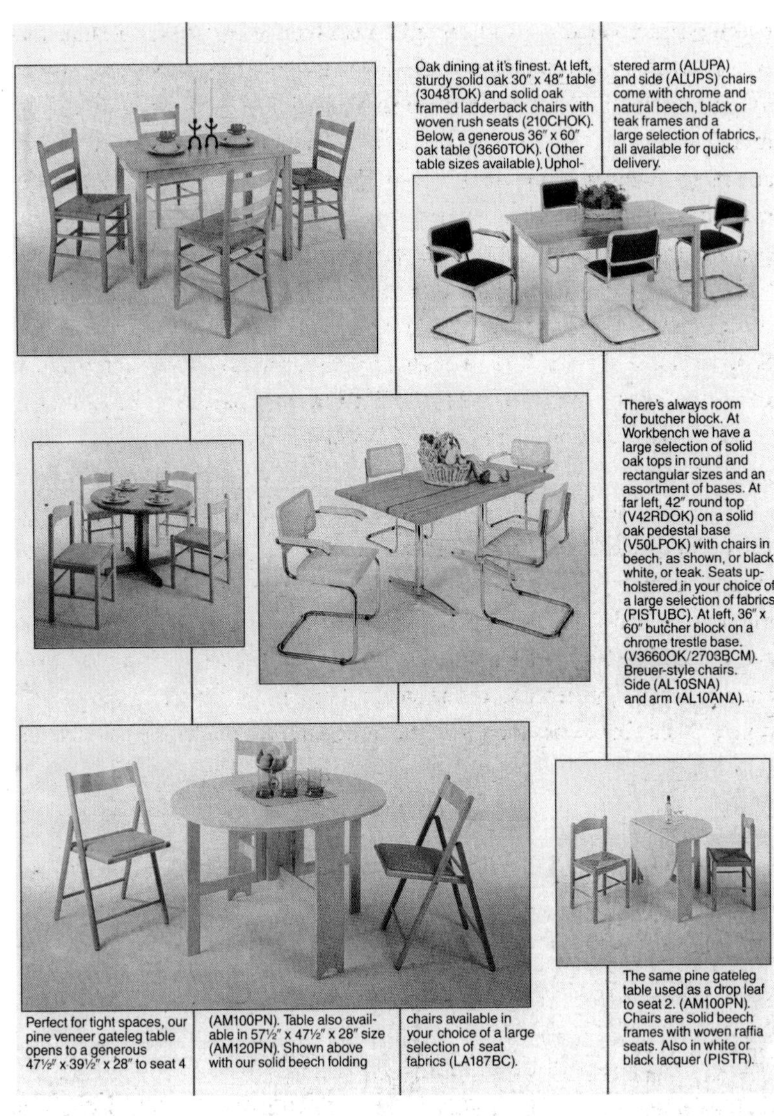

113 "A Consumer's Guide to Dining," brochure for Workbench (1990).

accommodations for cheaper production were justified, for "cutting cost is what Breuer wanted."[17] Similarly, in 1994, Mies's leather-upholstered "Barcelona" chair, still the most prestigious functionalist item, went for prices ranging from 890 dollars (virtually what the Knoll version sold for in 1964) to 3,800, although sale prices would have brought these figures down.

— Functionalism in its early definition as efficiency, economy, and utility also flourishes today. With mass merchandisers putting their weight behind lines of flexible, standardized, modular, mass-produced, and often knock-

114 The Museum of Modern Art's example of Ludwig Mies van der Rohe's "Barcelona" chair made by Knoll Associates by 1953 (fig. 90), after being reupholstered in white leather. Stainless steel and leather. Height 29 3/8" (75 cm). The Mies van der Rohe Archive, The Museum of Modern Art, New York. Gift of Knoll International.

down furniture, these practical items have become widely available. Habitat in Great Britain, Ikea from Sweden, and a group of outlets including the Workbench and the Doorstore in the United States sell such items in various grades of material and manufacture, often alongside lines of tubular-metal seating usually copied from or inspired by Breuer's "Cesca" chair. It takes little more than a glimpse at a catalogue or advertisement (fig. 113) to appreciate the lasting impact of the decade that gave us Weissenhof. But while these practical furnishings can make our lives more commodious at reasonable prices, it is the tubular-steel functionalist pieces of the 1920s that have entered our collective consciousness. These are the classics of our century. These are the works we study in art history classes, these are the ones we admire in museums. Regardless of how hackneyed they seem in everyday contexts, when we contemplate them in the calm of a gallery, they project the eternal values that functionalism sought to bring to our lives. The comfort and peace that is said to come with turning to the classics is not to be underestimated, and we should not be too ready to dismiss the sincerity of one of Mark Leyner's with-it heroes, a postmodern everyboy, when he draws solace from their aura. A condemned prisoner, he approaches his doom reciting the dogma of classic modernism: "Luckily, I'd developed an unusually close relationship with the warden. Knowing how much I loved Miës van der Rohe, he had an electric Barcelona chair custom-built for my execution. And when the date finally came and I was led into the death chamber, I couldn't help but marvel at the delicate curvature of the X-shaped legs, the perfect finish of the plated steel and the leather upholstery, and the magnificent, almost monumental proportions that have made the Barcelona chair timeless."[18]

Notes

1 Robert Venturi and Denise Scott Brown, "Functionalism, Yes, But," statement for the symposium "The Pathos of Functionalism," Berlin, 1974, in *Architecture and Urbanism* 47 (November 1974), pp. 33–34.

2 Vincent Scully, Introduction, in Robert Venturi, *Complexity and Contradiction in Architecture* (New York: The Museum of Modern Art, 1966), p. 13.

3 See David Whitney and Jeffrey Kipnis, eds., *Philip Johnson: The Glass House* (New York: Pantheon Books, 1993).

4 Philip Johnson, "Where Are We At?," [review of *Theory and Design in the First Machine Age*, by Reyner Banham], *Architectural Review* 127 (September 1960), pp. 174, 175.

5 See Charles A. Jencks, "Philip Johnson–The Candid King Midas of New York Camp," in *Late Modern Architecture and Other Essays* (New York: Rizzoli, 1980), pp. 146–59.

6 Reyner Banham, *Theory and Design in the First Machine Age* (London: The Architectural Press, 1960).

7 Reyner Banham, "A Throw-Away Esthetic," *Industrial Design* 7 (March 1960), p. 63.

8 Robert Venturi, *Complexity*, pp. 22–23.

9 See Charles F. Stuckey, "Scott Burton Chairs," in Jiri Svestka, ed., *Scott Burton: Sculptures 1980–89* (Düsseldorf: Kunstverein für die Rheinlande und Westfalen, 1989), pp. 55–65.

10 Pilar Viladas, "Corbusier Shows His True Colors," *Interiors* 139 (January 1980), pp. 120–21.

11 Ludwig Glaeser, *Ludwig Mies van der Rohe: Furniture and Furniture Drawings from the Design Collection and the Mies van der Rohe Archive* (New York: The Museum of Modern Art, 1977).

12 Martin Filler, "Seeing the Forest for the Trees," *Progressive Architecture* 58 (October 1977), p. 58.

13 European Furniture Importers, Chicago, catalogue, 1992.

14 See Véronique Vienne, "Furniture as Fashion: It's Not What You Wear, It's Where You Sit," *Metropolis* 12 (May 1993), pp. 65–67, 92–93.

15 See Carol Vogel, Currents: "Knockoff! Knockoff! Price Wars Are No Joke," *New York Times*, April 12, 1990, p. C3.

16 Elaine Louie, "The Many Lives of a Very Common Chair," *New York Times*, February 7, 1991, p. C10.

17 Warren Rubin, founder of the Workbench stores, quoted in ibid.

18 Mark Leyner, *My Cousin, My Gastroenterologist* (New York: Harmony Books, 1990), p. 32.

Selected Bibliography

Adolf G. Schneck, 1883–1971: Leben, Lehre, Möbel, Architektur. Stuttgart: Institut für Innenarchitektur und Möbel Design, 1983.

Banham, Reyner. *Theory and Design in the First Machine Age.* New York: The Architectural Press, 1960.

Benton, Tim, and Charlotte Benton, with Dennis Sharp, eds. *Form and Function: A Source Book for the History of Architecture and Design 1890–1939.* London: Crosby Lockwood Staples in association with the Open University Press, 1975.

Bonython, Elizabeth. *King Cole: A Picture Portrait of Sir Henry Cole, KCB 1808–1882.* London: Victoria and Albert Museum, 1982.

Brolin, Brent C. *Flight of Fancy: The Banishment and Return of Ornament.* New York: St. Martin's Press, 1985.

Buddensieg, Tilmann. *Industriekultur: Peter Behrens and the AEG, 1907–1914.* Cambridge, Mass., and London: The MIT Press, 1984.

—, ed. *Berlin 1900–1933: Architecture and Design.* New York and Berlin: Cooper Hewitt Museum and Gebr. Mann Verlag, 1987.

Burckhardt, Lucius, ed. *The Werkbund: History and Ideology, 1907–1933.* Woodbury, N.Y.: Barron's, 1980.

Campbell, Joan. *The German Werkbund: The Politics of Reform in the Applied Arts.* Princeton, N.J.: Princeton University Press, 1978.

Casteras, Susan P., and Ronald Parkinson, eds. *Richard Redgrave, 1804–1888.* New Haven and London: Yale University Press in association with the Victoria and Albert Museum and the Yale Center for British Art, 1988.

Collins, Michael, and Andreas Papadakis. *Post-Modern Design.* New York: Rizzoli, 1989.

De Zurko, Edward Robert. *Origins of Functionalist Theory.* New York: Columbia University Press, 1957.

Dieckmann, Erich. *Möbelbau in Holz, Rohr und Stahl.* Stuttgart: Julius Hofmann Verlag, 1931.

Droste, Magdalena. *Bauhaus, 1919–1933.* Cologne: Benedikt Taschen, 1993.

—, and Manfred Ludewig. *Marcel Breuer: Design.* Cologne: Benedikt Taschen, 1992.

Geest, Jan van, and Otakar Máčel. *Stühle aus Stahl: Metallmöbel, 1925–1940.* Cologne: Verlag der Buchhandlung Walther König, 1980.

Giedion, Siegfried. *Mechanization Takes Command: A Contribution to Anonymous History.* New York: Oxford University Press, 1948.

Glaeser, Ludwig. *Ludwig Mies van der Rohe: Furniture and Furniture Drawings from the Design Collection and the Mies van der Rohe Archive.* New York: The Museum of Modern Art, 1977.

Heskett, John. *German Design, 1870–1918.* New York: Taplinger Publishing Company, 1986.

Hiesinger, Kathryn B., and George H. Marcus. *Landmarks of Twentieth-Century Design.* New York: Abbeville Press, 1993.

Johnson, Philip. *Machine Art.* New York: The Museum of Modern Art and W. W. Norton and Company, 1934.

Kirsch, Karin. *The Weissenhofsiedlung: Experimental Housing Built for the Deutscher Werkbund, Stuttgart, 1927.* New York: Rizzoli, 1989.

Larrabee, Eric, and Massimo Vignelli. *Knoll Design.* New York: Harry N. Abrams Publishers, 1981.

Le Corbusier. *The Decorative Art of Today.* Translated by James I. Dunnett. Cambridge, Mass.: The MIT Press, 1981.

—. *Towards a New Architecture.* Translated by Frederick Etchells. London: John Rodker Publisher, 1927.

Lichtenstein, Claude. *Ferdinand Kramer: Der Charme des Systematischen.* Giessen, Germany: Anabas Verlag, 1991.

Lindinger, Herbert, ed. *Ulm Design, The Morality of Objects: Hochschule für Gestaltung Ulm 1953–1968.* Cambridge, Mass.: The MIT Press, 1991.

Möller, Werner, and Otakar Máčel. *Ein Stuhl macht Geschichte.* Munich: Prestel, 1992.

Musées de la Ville de Strasbourg. *L'Esprit Nouveau: Le Corbusier et l'industrie 1920–1925.* 1987.

Naylor, Gillian. *The Arts and Crafts Movement: A Study of Its Sources, Ideals, and Influence on Design Theory.* London: Studio Vista, 1971.

Neumann, Eckhard. *Bauhaus and Bauhaus People.* New York: Van Nostrand Reinhold Company, 1970.

Ostergard, Derek E., ed. *Bent Wood and Metal Furniture: 1850–1946.* New York: American Federation of Arts, 1987.

Pevsner, Nikolaus. *High Victorian Design: A Study of the Exhibits of 1851.* London: Architectural Press, 1951.

—. *Pioneers of Modern Design: From William Morris to Walter Gropius.* Rev. ed. Harmondsworth: Penguin Books, 1975.

Pommer, Richard, and Christian F. Otto. *Weissenhof 1927 and the Modern Movement in Architecture.* Chicago and London: The University of Chicago Press, 1991.

Schaefer, Herwin. *Nineteenth Century Modern: The Functional Tradition in Victorian Design.* New York and Washington, D.C.: Praeger Publishers, 1970.

Stansky, Peter. *Redesigning the World: William Morris, the 1880s, and the Arts and Crafts.* Princeton: Princeton University Press, 1985.

Troy, Nancy J. *Modernism and the Decorative Arts in France: Art Nouveau to Le Corbusier.* New Haven: Yale University Press, 1991.

Venturi, Robert. *Complexity and Contradiction in Architecture.* New York: The Museum of Modern Art, 1966.

Wilk, Christopher. *Marcel Breuer: Furniture and Interiors.* New York: The Museum of Modern Art, 1981.

—. *Thonet: 150 Years of Furniture.* Woodbury, N.Y., and London: Barron's, 1980.

Wilson, Richard Guy, Dianne H. Pilgrim, and Dickran Tashjian. *The Machine Age in America, 1918–1941.* New York: The Brooklyn Museum in association with Harry N. Abrams Publishers, 1986.

Wingler, Hans M. *The Bauhaus: Weimar Dessau Berlin Chicago.* Cambridge, Mass., and London: The MIT Press, 1969.

Photographic Acknowledgments

Photographs that were not taken from the author's or the publisher's archives were kindly provided by the following:

Albrecht Bangert, Munich: pl. 11

Photograph © 1995, The Art Institute of Chicago. All Rights Reserved: fig. 101

Bauhaus, Dessau: figs. 50, 68–69 (photo: Peter Kühn, 1988)

Bauhaus-Archiv, Berlin: pls. 2–3, 6; figs. 3, 46, 51, 53, 58

© The Trustees of The British Museum, London: pl. 1

Tilmann Buddensieg, Sinzig, Germany: fig. 16

Burg Giebichenstein, Hochschule für Kunst und Design, Halle/Saale: fig. 25 (photo: Reinhard Hentze)

Cassina S.p.A., Meda/Milan: pl. 19

Jean-Loup Charmet, Paris: fig. 20

Christie's Amsterdam: pl. 13

© Fondation Le Corbusier—Spadem, Paris: pl. 8; fig. 2

Fischer Fine Art, Ltd., London: pl. 9

Klaus Frahm, Hamburg: pl. 14

Hackman Designor, Iittala, Finland: fig. 93

The Knoll Group: pls. 15, 21; fig. 112

Library of Congress, Washington, D.C., Mies van der Rohe Archive: fig. 74

© 1995, The Limited, Inc., Columbus, Ohio: fig. 111

Atelier Mendini, Milan: pl. 18; fig. 104

The Metropolitan Museum of Art, New York: figs. 4, 6–8

Herman Miller Incorporated, Zeeland, Michigan: pl. 16

Musée d'Orsay, Paris: fig. 13 (© Photo R.M.N.)

Musée des Arts Décoratifs, Paris: fig. 40

Photographs © 1995, The Museum of Modern Art, New York: pl. 7; figs. 75–77 (Copy Print © 1995, The Mies van der Rohe Archive, The Museum of Modern Art, New York), 72, 79, 81, 84, 97, 99

Museum für Kunst und Gewerbe, Hamburg: fig. 103

National Diet Library, Tokyo: fig. 65

Die Neue Sammlung, Munich: figs. 1, 17, 30–31, 87, 108

© 1934, 1962 The New Yorker Magazine, Inc. All Rights Reserved/General Research Division, The New York Public Library, Astor, Lenox and Tilden Foundations, New York: fig. 83

The New York Public Library, Art and Architecture Collection, Marian and Ira D. Wallach Division of Art, Prints and Photographs, Astor, Lenox and Tilden Foundations, New York: figs. 78, 91–92

Philadelphia Museum of Art, Philadelphia: pl. 17; figs. 10, 12, 15, 22–24, 27, 32, 39

Photofest, New York: fig. 88

Max Protetch Gallery, New York: figs. 105, 107

Photograph © RCHME Crown Copyright: fig. 11

Staatliche Kunstsammlungen, Dresden: fig. 37

© 1995, Staatliche Museen zu Berlin, Preussischer Kulturbesitz Kunstgewerbemuseum, Berlin: pl. 4 (photo: Hans-Joachim Bertsch); figs. 26, 55

Victoria & Albert Museum, London: pl. 10; figs. 9, 70

Archiv Vitra Design Museum, Weil am Rhein: pl. 20; fig. 67

Zanotta S.p.A., Nova Milanese, Italy: fig. 109 (photo: Masera, Milan)

Index of Names